THE EDUCATION OF MOTOR AND
NEUROLOGICALLY HANDICAPPED CHILDREN

THE EDUCATION OF MOTOR AND NEUROLOGICALLY HANDICAPPED CHILDREN

Simon H. Haskell
Elizabeth K. Barrett
Helen Taylor

A HALSTED PRESS BOOK

CROOM HELM LONDON

JOHN WILEY & SONS
New York

© 1977 Simon H. Haskell, Elizabeth K. Barrett, Helen Taylor
Croom Helm, 2-10 St John's Road, London SW11

Published in the USA.
by Halsted Press, a Division
of John Wiley & Sons, Inc.
New York
British Library Cataloguing in Publication Data

Haskell, Simon H.
    The education of motor and neurologically
    handicapped children.
    1. Physically handicapped children —
    Education
    I. Title II. Barrett, Elizabeth K III. Taylor,
    Helen
    371.9'1   LC4215

    Croom Helm ISBN 0-85664-149-9
    Halsted ISBN 0 470-99276-X

Printed and bound in Great Britain

CONTENTS

ACKNOWLEDGEMENTS

This book would not have been possible without the help of a great many many friends and colleagues. Helen Taylor would like to acknowledge her debt to the late Arthur Maderson for his advice and inspiration. It is a pleasure to record our appreciation to Barbara Smith and Val Blick for their cheerful and willing help in typing some draft chapters. We owe a special debt of gratitude to Heather Nankervis for the untiring and meticulous care she devoted to its organisation and for typing the entire manuscript, and we would also like to thank Peter Nankervis, who was kind enough to provide the excellent drawings.

We are deeply grateful to the Yooralla Hospital for Crippled Children for their generous assistance in donating their photographic facilities. Our warm thanks go to Geoffrey Say, Executive Director of Yooralla for his encouragement and interest, and to Sister Addison for her invaluable help in selecting the children and giving clinical background information.

Others have given invaluable help by their careful reading of several chapters and for helpful corrections and comments. These include Audrey King and Neil Taylor, who both gave general help of all types; Betty Sutcliffe, Joan Kell and Thomas M. Barrett. We are grateful to Dr Herbert Goldstein for commenting so helpfully on the final chapter, and offer thanks to Harold Stubbings, formerly of the Cambridge University Press, for proof-reading the manuscript and for preparing the index. To our publishers we offer our appreciation for all their help, interest and encouragement.

PREFACE

This book has been written in response to requests made over the last ten years by teachers taking the course for the University of London Diploma in the Education of Physically Handicapped Children. In addition there have been requests by psychologists, therapists, doctors and others working with physically handicapped children.

Books dealing with our particular subject are few and it is hoped that this contribution may help in the identification of some of the problems that, as Nicholas Hobbs puts it, 'can blight the life of a child, reduce opportunity, diminish his competence and self-esteem, alienate him from others, nurture a meanness of spirit, and make him less a person than he could become'.

We hope this book will increase the understanding of the difficulties encountered by neurologically impaired and physically handicapped children by those privileged to work with them. Furthermore we hope it may influence public policy in continuing to improve educational services for the physically handicapped.

We have discussed only a few topics but we have attempted to crystallise thinking on some of the effects of neurological and motor disabilities on learning. We could well have chosen other topics but would then have run the risk of attempting to cover too wide a field thereby oversimplifying the issues. We have made no attempt to cover all the literature connected with our subject; instead we have directed our attention to that which is most pertinent to our theme.

The book is divided into four sections. In Section I we describe the development of the normal child and the procedures for evaluating his physical condition. This is followed by an account of some handi-capping conditions which often lead to special school placement.

Section II describes some of the psychological consequences of motor and neurological impairment and especially the disorders of learning, perception and motor ability that arise as a result.

In Section III we have attempted to analyse the causes and nature of difficulties of the children under discussion in the basic school, subjects of Reading, Spelling, Handwriting and Arithmetic and, where appropriate, have described some measures undertaken to remedy these weaknesses.

In the final section there is a discussion of the social and community arrangements for educating handicapped children in England and Wales, Hungary and the United States of America. A description of these contrasting approaches may help the reader to appreciate the historical and socio-cultural forces behind the present day education of physically handicapped children.

Lionel Penrose's prophetic remarks about the importance of mentally handicapped people today is equally true of persons suffering from neurological impairment. Penrose declared at the 1960 International Conference on the study of mental deficiency:

> The time is now at hand when mentally retarded children are likely to become very important people. Paediatricians are scrambling over one another to investigate the medical problems presented by them. . . moreover, these formerly despised individuals have at last become of a positive interest to the biologist. . . . mentally handicapped individuals can reveal, unwittingly, information of the utmost value to the rest of the community and we well may be grateful to them for this service.

We believe that children with neurological and motor disabilities can similarly improve our knowledge of normal children and their development, especially as research evidence of the behaviour of handicapped children becomes available.

SECTION 1 : MEDICAL ISSUES

The aim of this section is to enable to reader to have some understanding of the medical aspects/background of a physically handicapped child. A description is given of normal physical development, as tested in standa standard medical examinations of young children. We have chosen this method of approach because it is the failure to obtain the expected norm that reveals disability in a child. A brief simple description follows of various physically handicapping conditions which are currently making it necessary for children to receive 'special' education of some kind. Readers are referred to the Glossary at the end of the book for technical terms not explained in the text.

1 NORMAL CHILD DEVELOPMENT AND ASSESSMENT PROCEDURES

From his first moments of life, a child is rated in terms of success or failure according to criteria adopted by the society into which he is born. In our own society those initial criteria are medical. The new-born child can be assessed in terms of his health by means of the Apgar test, which rates his physical condition on arrival in the world.

Even before this, throughout a woman's pregnancy, the health service has provided standard antenatal care at a hospital, clinic or from the local general practitioner to ensure, as far as possible, the normal development of the child from conception to birth. Monthly, and eventually weekly, examinations of the expectant mother are undertaken to monitor the baby's development and the mother's health. In particular, her blood pressure is checked to note early signs of toxaemia of pregnancy. Special care is recommended to avoid exposure to infectious diseases, for example rubella (German measles), which, if contracted, may damage the developing baby by causing mental retardation or other disabilities.

The maintenance of good health and adequate nutrition is important to the mother and her child. The family history of both parents is noted to check for any past physical or mental diseases, and the history of previous pregnancies or miscarriages is recorded. Thus the baby who is 'at risk' from conception can be identified.

The Apgar test, administered within minutes of a baby's birth, assesses the heart rate, the respiratory effort (in terms of the cry) and muscle tone (in terms of the flexion of the limbs), the response of the baby's skin to stimulation (known as reflex irritability) and the colour of the baby, whether bluish or a healthy pink. The full score of ten shows the normal healthy baby.

The new-born baby's score on the Apgar test may well be affected by the process of birth, and his first response to life is a useful indication of what, if any, his immediate treatment should be, and how he is likely to progress subsequently. Any of the following factors might affect the Apgar test result:

1. the baby is premature;
2. labour has been long and difficult;
3. there was a multiple birth;

4. delivery was Caesarian, breach or required forceps;
5. there was any temporary cut-off in the oxygen supply to the baby;
6. drugs were used to aid delivery.

A low score can help to predict the liability of death or permanent cerebral damage in a child.

Following this test, in the next few days, a full medical examination of the baby will take place. The doctor assesses the baby's reflexes, weighs him, takes measurements of his body and the circumference of his head, examines his eyes and the abduction of his hips. The primitive reflexes present in babies up to about the first six months, and which indicate a normal neurological condition, include:

1. the Moro reflex, in which the baby's arms and legs extend when its head is allowed to fall back.
2. the sucking and swallowing reflex;
3. the rooting reflex, whereby a touch at the side of the baby's mouth causes it to turn and seek the nipple;
4. the grasp reflex, that is, the fingers gripping an object placed in the baby's palm;
5. the placing reflex, where the baby's foot steps up on to the table if first held up against the table edge;
6. the stepping reflex, where the baby's feet 'walk' along the ground when placed on a surface; and
7. the asymmetric tonic reflex, in which the baby's right side limbs extend and the left flex, when his face is turned to the right, and vice versa.

From early life, therefore, the child's health and development are checked against an expected norm to obtain warning of developmental delays or more serious motor and neurological damage. This assessment continues at infant welfare clinics throughout the first five years of life, under the supervision of the health visitor or child health personnel responsible for the area, who are assigned to every family from the birth of a new child, and the paediatrician who sees the child regularly at the clinic.

Developmental assessment is a part of preventive medicine designed to detect any problems in a child and chart his progress in the early years. It is dependent for its success upon the co-operation of parents, the efficiency of health visitors and doctors and the accuracy and standardisation of the procedures used. Illingworth (1972) has pointed out the mistakes and pitfalls in developmental diagnosis and writes:

> Developmental diagnosis can only be made on the basis of carefully
> detailed history, a full developmental, neurological and physical
> examination, and particularly in the light of others who have warned
> everyone that developmental diagnosis demands the greatest
> diagnostic acumen, common sense and caution.

The general procedure at developmental screening sessions includes:

1. discussion with the mother about any problems of feeding, sleeping
or behaviour in the child;
2. any illnesses affecting mother or child;
3. any family or environmental changes, such as a change in the
father's job or perhaps moving house.

The paediatrician usually has some equipment for testing the child,
which is the next step in the proceedings. This includes things like tissue
paper, a bell and a rattle for testing hearing, white balls of different
sizes for testing visual acuity, cubes for stacking and grasping, and
familiar toys for older infants to assess the level of language development.
There is also a physical examination. According to his findings, the
paediatrician can then recommend a course of action for a particular
child. By comparing the baby with others of the same age and with their
average performance, his rate of development can be assessed and his
developmental potential predicted. More important, severe or moderate
mental subnormality or the presence of cerebral palsy, as well as visual
and hearing defects, can be diagnosed. Muscle tone can be assessed and
neurological defects also diagnosed, but intelligence cannot be tested or
accurately predicted. While some young children may not show signs of
mild mental subnormality or cerebral palsy, the possibility of later
learning disorders in such children cannot be excluded.
    Developmental assessment usually takes place at six weeks, six
months, ten months, eighteen months, two, three and four-and-a-half
years. As children vary greatly in their development, the following
'milestones', as they are sometimes called, are only approximate, and
the paediatrician would not be worried by a single delay in a child's
progress. Rather, he looks for a 'cluster' of delays or abnormalities as
a sign that all is not as it should be.

Neonatal Period

In the first three to four months, the absence of the primitive reflexes
referred to earlier, or their continuation beyond that period, may
indicate cerebral damage or delay. Asymmetry in the Moro reflex or
in 'walking', or tightly closed fists after two months are examples of
what the doctor looks for.

From about the fourth to the seventh month, other responses occur
in the normal baby. Examples are the rolling responses, where if the
head is rotated the body follows it round, and various protective
reactions such as the 'parachute' reflex in which the arms stretch
forward if the baby is tilted towards the ground, or the head remains
erect (balancing reaction) as the body changes position in space. This
reaction is absent or partially present in children with cerebral palsy.
Apart from the reflexes, the expected pattern of development in the
six-week-old baby includes the presence of reasonable head control,
responses to visual and auditory stimuli, and the beginning of smiling
back and gazing at mother. Problems the doctor looks for are difficulties
in sucking or swallowing, undue sleepiness, irritability or crying, and
any factors at home causing stress to mother or child. Prematurity or
post-natal illness such as jaundice may delay these 'milestones', but
more serious signs of abnormal development include restricted hip
abduction, an unusually large or small head, asymmetry of movements,
tone and reflexes, head lag or low/high muscle tone (the floppy/stiff
baby).

Six Months

By now the primitive reflexes have gone, the baby has good head
control, is interested in the visual and auditory stimuli presented by
the paediatrician, can almost sit unsupported, can raise head and chest
off the couch when prone, can roll over, is socially responsive, fixates
well visually, and smiles frequently. He has 'found' his hands and begins
to transfer objects between them. He is able to chew, to vocalise, to
show excitement at the approach of food, or protest at the removal of
a toy; he holds his hands out to be picked up, coughs to attract
attention, and begins to imitate his parents.

Indications of cerebral damage, or delays, will show in various
ways, viz. the lack of alertness in the baby, visual defects, tightly
closed hands, head lag and abnormal head size. It is also shown in the
inability:

1. to support his weight on his feet, or
2. fix his gaze on a pellet, or
3. grasp a brick, or
4. hear the tissue paper, the rattle of the spoon in a cup and turn to it.

Ten Months

At about ten months the baby is usually mobile, able to roll, to crawl, and to pull up to standing. He uses his index finger to explore objects, he has a pincer grasp (thumb and first finger), follows falling objects, vocalises widely and imitates well. He objects to strangers and is aware of the difference in individuals. He sits well, by now unsupported, and he may walk holding on to furniture. Perhaps he can say 'Mummmm' or 'Dada', wave bye-bye, feed himself a biscuit, chew solids and babble a lot in play.

Doubt as to development would be felt if the infant had had any convulsions, still had an abnormally sized head, could not bear his weight on his legs, showed low or high muscle tone, if he were backward in manipulating objects with his hands, if he were poor in vision or hearing, if he failed to respond to vocalising, and smiled or laughed very little. Unusually static limbs or ataxia (tremor) in reaching for objects would also indicate damage or delay.

Eighteen Months

The child is now highly active; he responds to objects all around him; he shows simple constructive abilities, has good verbal comprehension, says several familiar words, and begins to show some obstructive behaviour as independence is gained. He usually makes his wants known by pointing and naming simple objects. From thirteen months he will have been walking; he can feed himself and drink from a cup without spilling the contents; he copies mother's domestic activities, and he is beginning to be toilet trained. Girls are usually more advanced than boys at this stage.

The paediatrician would consider referring the child to a specialist if, at this stage, he drools, casts down objects, is unsteady in gait, cannot build with bricks or cannot respond to simple commands or speak any words clearly.

Two Years

Now extremely independent, the child walks, runs, climbs, attempts activities for himself but needs the support of adults, communicates well and expresses his own ideas. Points to be checked are the presence of two-or-three word sentences, the understanding of instructions, the ability to play with a toy, the ability to feed and dress himself, and to note if he is beginning to stay clean and dry. The paediatrician checks responsiveness to pictures in books, to the offer of a pencil, to the copying of a bridge of bricks, and to awareness of the parts of the body. He also ensures that hearing and sight are in order.

Three Years

Now quicker in his movements, enthusiastic in jumping, climbing, attempting to throw and catch a ball, the child has increased in security and can tolerate being left for short periods. He still needs familiar adult surroundings. He plays imaginatively and enjoys playing in company with other children but sharing things with them is still difficult. Speech is well established. The paediatrician will assess the child's ability to stand on one foot, build a cube tower, copy a simple bridge construction, copy a circle, match colours, identify useful objects, and he will also test the child's ability to recognise letters.

At this stage the paediatrician would be concerned by aimless over-activity on the part of the child, or failure to talk in sentences or indistinct speech.

Four-and-a-half Years

The child can now skip, hop, ride a tricycle and play with other children. He can understand ideas of sharing and taking turns, indulge in make-believe play and produce clear thinking speech in long sentences. The paediatrician will check for tremor, for the child's ability to dress himself, his general alertness, his relationships with others and his behaviour when alone. He will also repeat the shape copying mentioned earlier and the construction of a bridge. Vision and hearing are tested, and a reasonable conversation between doctor and child is expected.

The School-Age Child

Once the child is of school age and has for any reason to be seen by a doctor, the information about him is extensive. His developmental history, as outlined above, has been recorded, and the doctor examining him can also refer if necessary to any history of disease or ill health in the family. In addition, physical examinations of the vital systems are carried out — heart and peripheral circulation, the lungs and upper respiratory tracts. At the same time, the nose and throat are considered and a check of the ears is usually made (ear infections being commonly associated with upper respiratory tract infections).

Direct questioning may aid the actual physical investigation of the stomach and alimentary system. Any abnormalities of other abdominal organs, such as the spleen and liver, may be detected by a physical examination. Similarly, some conditions of the kidneys and genito-urinary system may also be identified.

Further systematic measurements of height and weight and other indicators of physical growth may be useful. A more detailed examination of the central nervous system may be indicated in children exhibiting problems such as poor co-ordination.

In conclusion, it should be emphasised that the most important aspects of a child's development are his alertness, his powers of concentration, his determination and his interest in his surroundings. These are functions the paediatrician finds difficult to assess. But if a proper history is taken and the child is seen at regular intervals, a great deal in the way of prediction and prevention can be achieved.

2 HANDICAPPING CONDITIONS

Once a child has been diagnosed as suffering from a particular handicap, the condition, its cause (if known), its treatment (if any), and special education facilities need clarification for the parents, the child and the teachers involved.

This chapter describes briefly most of the common handicapping conditions to be found in schools for the physically handicapped (cerebral palsy – CP, epilepsy, hydrocephalus, spina bifida and muscular dystrophy), and in lesser detail, other handicapping conditions such as scoliosis, cystic fibrosis, thalidomide, haemophilia, polio, heart disease, asthma and juvenile rheumatoid arthritis (Still's disease).

If we take Jolly's (1954) definition of a handicapped child as 'one suffering from any continuing disability of body, intellect or personality which is likely to interfere with his normal growth, development or capacity to learn', the strictly medical definitions which this section employs must be seen as only one aspect of the child. Furthermore, many children suffer from a number of conditions, and emotional and psychiatric disorders may result from these in addition to the medically diagnosed handicap. It is more realistic to assemble a full picture of a handicapped child based on medical, social, psychological and educational records, and to recognise the great degree of overlap between these aspects.

Cerebral Palsy

'Cerebral Palsy (CP) is a disorder of movement and posture resulting from a permanent, non-progressive defect or lesion of the immature brain' (Bax, 1964). The motor aspects of the disorder are usually accompanied by defects of sight or hearing, speech and intellect, as well as abnormal behaviour patterns. Although the condition is non-progressive, its manifestations may alter.

The cause of the condition may occur in the pre-natal period, for example, the mother may transmit some kind of congenital malformation of the brain, or some infection. Or a combination of pre-natal and perinatal factors, such as rhesus incompatibility, together with a certain level of hyperbilirubinaemia can develop after birth, which produces kernicterus and may result in a particular type of cerebral palsy, athetosis. Perinatal factors such as prematurity, injury at birth, or anoxia (a cut-off in the supply of oxygen to the baby's brain) may also cause CP. Hypoglycaemia, which occurs when the blood glucose in the baby falls below 40 mg per cent, usually the result of toxaemia in the pregnancy, is a further cause. In the post-natal period, infections of the brain such as meningitis and encephalitis may result in CP. Trauma, too, is a possible cause.

The three major kinds of CP are classified as spasticity, athetosis and ataxia, although there may be mixed types.

Figure 1. Areas of the brain which, when damaged, cause the different forms of cerebral palsy.

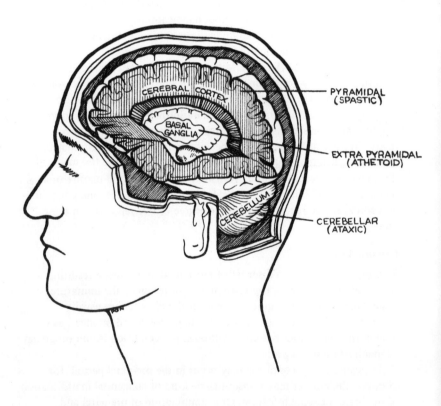

Spasticity affects about 60 per cent of the CP population and is the most common of the three types. It is due to a pyramidal lesion (the neuron in the motor cortex which is damaged is shaped like a pyramid, hence the name), and is diagnosed as an increase in muscle tone or hypertonicity. The limbs involved are stiff but weak and have a muscle imbalance. This means that one set of muscles is contracting too much, whereas the other corresponding set is too weak to withstand the contractions. The spastic shows reflex activity which is higher than normal and abnormal postures, and the condition is maintained during sleep. Various limbs are affected by the disorder. Partial paralysis of one limb is known as monoplegia, although (according to Jolly), this may be an incorrect diagnosis, since the condition usually reveals the presence of hemiplegia or paraplegia on closer study. Hemiplegia involves paralysis of two limbs on the same side of the body, the arm being more affected than the leg. Speech and intelligence may also be affected, and convulsions are common. The limbs on the affected side grow more slowly. Triplegia means that three limbs are affected and tetraplegia means the involvement of four limbs. Paraplegia is present when both legs are affected though the face and hands are normal, in which case speech is not affected, intelligence is often normal, and convulsions are rare. However, many patients are found to have mild involvement of the upper limbs also, thus being strictly defined as diplegics. Diplegia is present when all four limbs are affected and the legs are worse than the arms. The two halves of the body are affected symmetrically, unlike double hemiplegia. Several mental defects and convulsions are common in diplegia. Double hemiplegia affects all four limbs, the arms being more affected than the legs. In addition, there is usually severe mental retardation.

A more detailed picture of the spastic hemiplegic would show the following pattern of development: delays in sitting, walking and talking at the infant stage, and subsequently learning and perceptual disorders at school. Physical development would include the shortness of one leg, an inturned hip, a flexed elbow and wrist, and contracture and atrophy of the muscles due to non-use. Bony growth on one side would be less. The spastic hemiplegic child may have multiplicity of handicaps, such as low intelligence, motor difficulties, sensory deficits, convulsions, speech difficulties, problems of vision and hearing, behaviour and personality disorders, respiratory difficulties and contractures, apart from having to cope with greater pressures of school and home life than would an unhandicapped child. Spastic hemiplegics are by far the largest group in the CP population, comprising 40 per cent.

Athetosis, the second major kind of CP, is characterised by increased involuntary and unco-ordinated movements, which may be slow and writhing or dramatically jerky. These movements do not occur in sleep or when the child is relaxed, but are always grossly exaggerated when a voluntary movement is attempted. Attempting to prevent this involuntary movement may also produce severe muscle tension in the child. The persistence of the primary reflexes, such as the asymmetrical tonic reflex and the Moro reflex, often accompany the disorder, and the muscles involving speech are often affected, producing a condition known as dysarthria. Intelligence, however, is usually normal. There may also be high-tone deafness, and, unlike spastic children, athetoid children are often thin, because of their excessive movements. The damage to the brain in the case of athetosis is extrapyramidal, the part affected being the basal ganglia.

Ataxia is possibly of hereditary origin and affects only a small number of children. The condition affects the arms, preventing precise movements and giving the appearance of clumsiness, or it affects the legs, causing an unsteady trembling gait, but sometimes all four limbs are involved, the legs more so than the arms. Damage to the cerebellum is the cause and the ataxic child fails to integrate the information relevant to its position and balance in space. Nystagmus and tremor are also present. This condition tends to improve as the child grows older.

Other terminology associated with CP includes:

1. 'hypotonia', which is often used in reference to athetoids and indicates a decrease in muscle tone; 'hypertonicity', mentioned earlier in connection with the spastic form of CP and referring to increased muscle tone;
2. 'rigidity', which is a term applied to spastic CP involving a stiffness over all the muscles affected; and
3. 'flaccidity', which is caused by a pyramidal lesion and produces increased tendon reflexes.

The importance of early and accurate diagnosis of the various conditions described here cannot be too strongly emphasised, as treatment may be successfully applied and deformities of the limbs prevented. The clinical classification of a particular child's condition should also be made known in some detail to the teachers and physiotherapists responsible for him. It has been found, for example, that approximately 25 per cent of hemiplegics also have a loss of vision in either the left eye or right half of the visual fields of both eyes (Tizard, Paine and Crothers, 1954). This clearly may interfere with normal reading. Tizard also showed that approximately 50 per cent of hemiplegics have an associated sensory impairment of the involved side, so that the child is unable to recognise an object by touch, and has a diminished sense of light touch or pain. The child may have a 'blind' limb, more useless than a motor handicapped limb. Such information may indicate the type of application of physiotherapy suitable for the child.

Treatment for CP may be of three kinds; surgical and non-surgical orthopaedic treatment, the use of drugs, and the application of physiotherapy. It is recommended that surgery be delayed until adolescence, when growth has ceased. Although drugs intended to relax the muscles in the CP child are usually of little benefit, they may be administered whilst physiotherapy is applied. Non-surgical orthopaedic treatment includes bracing or, in the case of spasticity, the wearing of casts to prevent contractures. Surgery to help a spastic child includes the correction of bony deformities, tendon and muscle releases or elongations, the neurectomies, where the nerves causing spasticity are temporarily paralysed. The major form of treatment, however, is continuous physiotherapy from the time the condition is diagnosed. Whichever approach is adopted, the aim is to increase the child's mobility, to enable him to have as many of the normal explorative and locomotive experiences of the growing child as possible, and to vary muscle tone, increasing and decreasing it where necessary. The physiotherapist tries to improve posture and enable the child to walk with or without support; he also provides exercises to prevent contractures. The occupational therapist, and also the physiotherapist, in most cases, concentrate on manipulative skills relevant to everyday needs. Toileting, eating, dressing and undressing can thus become the child's responsibility, and not another adult's. Therapy may extend into the classroom, where help in using a special typewriter may be given. Parental involvement and instruction is usually encouraged by the therapists, but discussion here of some of the types of physiotherapy treatment currently successfully in use cannot do justice to their methods. The Bobath approach is probably the most widely adopted, and the Peto system of conductive education is described elsewhere in the book in considerable detail. When a CP child has speech impairment, another important part of his treatment may involve the speech therapist, though severe damage to the muscles relevant to speech cannot be treated by formal speech therapy.

As a postscript to the various treatments, the abnormal patterns of behaviour frequently associated with CP children, which are considered organic, must be mentioned. These include hyperactivity, emotional lability, attentional peculiarities (short attention span or perseveration), low frustration tolerance, impulsivity and distractibility. These are discussed in greater detail elsewhere. Family counselling can help to stabilise these behaviours, and the use of drugs may also be thought appropriate in some instances. Behavioural psychology can also be employed to modify or eliminate undesirable behaviour.

Epilepsy

Epilepsy can be described as a paroxysmal and transitory disturbance of the function of the brain, which develops suddenly, ceases spontaneously, and has a tendency to recur. Its manifestations are a loss of concentration or consciousness, which may be accompanied by involuntary movements of the body. What we believe takes place is some spontaneous neuronic excitation at a point in the brain. This local discharge may spread and ultimately produce excitation of the sub-cortical centres concerned in the production of the generalised electrical disturbance of the brain. The nature of the appearance and spread of an epileptic discharge in the central nervous system appears to be intimately related to changes of a chemical and electrical nature at the cell membranes.

The difficulties of describing and classifying epilepsy are due to the lack of any absolute knowledge of what causes a fit. Distinctions are made between epilepsy, which is symptomatic of some underlying cause, such as brain injury or disease, and that which is idiopathic, where no organic cause is found but there may be genetic factors operating for the condition. There are different ways of classifying the condition:

1. according to the motor manifestations of the fit or seizure;
2. by differentiating between general and partial seizures;
3. by dividing it according to its anatomical location;
4. by its aetiology if known.

Jolly (ibid.), states,

In the absence of further knowledge, an open mind must be kept regarding the aetiology of fits and no satisfaction should be derived from the application of descriptive labels, even though these are required in order to discuss the subject. Above all, it should be realised that 'epilepsy' is not a diagnosis but a symptom whose cause must be determined.

The following are the common ways of classifying the seizure disorders.

Febrile Convulsions

These occur in the infant stage, last for a short period of time, and are usually associated with a rapid rise in temperature due to illness. Genetic factors play a large part in these convulsions. There is no means of distinguishing these fits from the *grand mal* kind occurring in idiopathic epilepsy, apart from awareness of the precipitating cause.

Symptomatic Convulsions

These are due to intracranial injury at birth or infections of the brain, such as meningitis or encephalitis. Any form of intracranial disorder can also cause these fits. So, too, may poisoning from lead or iron. The fit is focal and there may be some paralysis, either temporary or persistent.

Idiopathic Epilepsy

Grand Mal There are four stages in the attack, aura, tonic phase, clonic phase and stupor. Sometimes the child can anticipate the fit by the onset of a headache, a tired feeling, or even a feeling of fear. The convulsion is initiated by a loss of consciousness, the child may fall, the eyes roll upwards and respiration cease momentarily. At this point rhythmic movements of the extremities and face occur, though the arms and legs remain rigid. This may last minutes or continue, in rare cases, for some hours. Finally, the child becomes relaxed, moans and begins to move spontaneously. Sleep often follows. Incontinence of urine may occur in the attack and the tongue or lip may be bitten.

Status Epilepticus This term is applied to a series of rapidly recurring *grand mal* attacks without intervals of consciousness.

Petit Mal This form of attack arises in children between the years of three and nine, and rarely after the age of fifteen. There is a momentary loss of consciousness without any convulsive movements, no aura and no after-effect. The child may stop talking, stare into space, his eyelids may flutter but he does not fall. He may lose colour briefly and sway a little, but then continue as though nothing has happened. Urine may be passed. Attacks can be brought on by hyperventilation (deep breathing) or by photic stimulation. Mental retardation often accompanies the condition although sufferers can be highly intelligent. Frequent seizures can interfere with memory.

Myoclonus There is a sudden spasm of a muscle or group of muscles, without loss of consciousness, and this may occur in patients with *grand mal* or *petit mal,* or alone.

Temporal Lobe Epilepsy This form of attack begins with an abnormal discharge from the temporal lobe, producing hallucinations of smell and taste, with the child complaining of stomach discomfort or headache at the onset of the seizure. This is followed by unusual movements of the tongue, smacking of the lips or some repetitive motor movement. The child may be frightened and seek the comfort of someone near. During the few moments of the seizure, signs of perspiration, salivation, pallor or blushing and a rapid pulse occur. In some of these children a lesion has been found in the temporal lobe, which may be due to scarring following birth trauma. Accompanying this condition is an abnormal pattern of behaviour, where the child tends to be hyperkinetic, easily distracted, and has a short attention span. There are also rapid changes of mood, with aggressive tendencies or temper tantrums, and little sign of fear or shyness. Intelligence can be normal, though some children are mentally retarded.

Treatment

The major form of treatment for epilepsy is the administration of appropriate anticonvulsant drugs which control the seizures and enable the child to lead as normal a life as possible. Appropriate dosage suppresses the fits continually without producing negative side-effects. Overactivity in the temporal lobe form of epilepsy, for example, may be the result of an unsuitable drug, thereby worsening the hyperkinesis already present. Too much medication can also produce drowsiness, lack of co-ordination, double vision, and generally lower the level of the child's intellectual functioning. A proper combination of anticonvulsants can, however, increase intellectual efficiency.

In addition to medication reducing emotional and physiological stress for the child, encouraging parents and educationalists to recognise the condition without fear, and to try, where possible, not to overprotect the child can also help minimise the personality problems of the condition. Jolly says that:

> psychological disturbances are common in the epileptic patient, but the more these are investigated, the more it is apparent that they are the result of the environment and the way the child is handled, rather than the fits themselves. Most children with epilepsy have

normal personalities but their parents and some of their teachers find
great difficulty in handling them in a normal balanced manner.

Finally, a note on the electro encephalogram (EEG), a 'brain-wave'
test carried out on some epileptics. This test is employed by the
physician to help confirm his diagnosis of the condition, in conjunction
with other tests on the blood, or an X-ray of the skull. EEGs can prove
difficult to interpret, except when used by highly experienced neurologists. It is useful, as a regular record of a patient's condition, to study
the causes and kinds of fit and act as a developmental check, but, as it
only records fits occurring in the top centimetres of the brain, those
generated lower down may pass unnoticed.

Other terminology associated with epilepsy includes:

1. the Jacksonian or focal fit – infantile spasms occurring between
six months and two years;
2. akinetic seizures – in which no movements are apparent but the
child drops to the floor;
3. lobectomy – which is surgery to remove scarred tissue in the brain
that may be causing seizures.

Fifty per cent of children with CP have epilepsy as well. The best
pattern of medication may only be achieved by doctors and those caring
for children exchanging information fully and freely.

Hydrocephalus

Hydrocephalus may occur in association with spina bifida or independ-
ently, and is present when there is too much cerebrospinal fluid in the
ventricles of the brain. As the brain is soft, the ventricles enlarge with
the pressure of fluid, the brain tissue becomes thin and stretched, and
eventually permanent damage is caused.

In a small baby the bones at the top of the head are not joined
together and the excess fluid pushes them apart, allowing the head to
become much bigger. This symptom indicates the presence of hydrocephalus. The onset of the condition in older children or adults is
likely to lead to a more severe disturbance of the brain because the
bones of the head are no longer pliable.

The obstruction to the normal circulation of cerebrospinal fluid
may be because:

1. the brain may have developed abnormally;

2. there has been a severe infection of the brain, such as
meningitis, which causes changes in the cerebrospinal fluid
pathways;
3. of a brain haemorrhage, at birth, or in the neonatal period
or subsequently;
4. of the presence of a lump or cyst in the brain, which, according
to its position, may cause an obstruction.

If the condition is mild, no treatment may be thought necessary, but
the patient must remain under observation to prevent deterioration.
Any severe case requires some form of operation to direct the accumu-
lating fluid away from the distended ventricles, through a tube from
the ventricles to the atrium of the heart (an operation known as a
ventriculo-atrial shunt) where it is absorbed into the blood stream. The
ventriculo-peritoneal shunt directs the fluid to the peritoneal cavity,
which is the space surrounding the intestines, and works on the same
kind of principle. A spino-peritoneal shunt directs the fluid from the
ventricles to the space around the spinal cord and from there to the
peritoneal cavity.

Once such an operation has been performed the child has to be
seen regularly, so that, as he grows, the tube that has been inserted may
be lengthened accordingly. On rare occasions, the pump which is
attached to the tube may become blocked and require manipulating by
hand. There is also the risk of an infection occurring when a 'foreign
body' such as the tube has been inserted. In this event, drugs or the
temporary removal of the tube may be necessary. Most of the time,
however, the child can be allowed to lead a normal life with no special
attention necessary, and no restriction in activity because of the
inserted tube.

The prognosis for this condition varies according to its severity when
first treated. If the condition was mild in the first place, and no significant brain or associated disease followed, intelligence and physical
development should be in the normal range. A large head and wide
popping eyes, together with a rather happy, talkative disposition and
facile behaviour may characterise the condition. If there is associated
brain damage, spasticity or mental retardation may be present, despite
the treatment here described.

Spina Bifida

The term 'spina bifida' means literally 'a spine which is split or divided'.
In a baby with this condition, at one part of the spine one or more

vertebrae are not completely formed. In normal vertebrae there is a 'canal' through the centre containing the spinal cord, which houses the nerves connecting the brain to various parts of the body. When there is a split in the vertebrae this central canal is not complete at the level of the split, and it is, therefore, possible for the spinal cord and its coverings to protrude through the opening, causing a lump on the baby's back. The disruption and damage to the nerves at this point mean that the messages between the brain and the trunk and limbs are impaired, causing paralysis. Messages from the body to the brain indicating sensations of touch, pain and position are also blocked. The split in the vertebrae may occur at any point in the spine, although usually it is found at the lower end.

Spina bifida is genetically determined, and there is a one-in-twelve risk of the condition recurring in subsequent pregnancies following the birth of a spina bifida child. It is now possible to test for spina bifida at an early stage of pregnancy. There is, in fact, a greater incidence of anencephaly in the families of children with spina bifida than in the normal population.

The most common form of spina bifida is myelocele, or meningomyelocele, which occurs in the lumbar region, and is often associated with an Arnold-Chiari malformation, giving rise to hydrocephalus. Apart from paralysis of the legs and loss of sensation, the nerve supply to the sphincters is affected, causing incontinence of the bladder and bowel. Another form of spina bifida is meningocele, in which a sac, composed of the meninges, protrudes between the vertebrae in the neck or upper back, but the cord remains within the spinal canal and the overlying skin is usually normal. In some cases of meningocele, there is paralysis, loss of sensation and incontinence. If associated hydrocephalus is present in spina bifida an excess of fluid collects in the brain (due to a blockage in circulation), and under its pressure the child's head becomes progressively larger, and the brain compressed and damaged. This added complication to spina bifida may occur at birth or in the first six months of life, but is unlikely to develop thereafter. Other abnormalities occurring may be club-foot (or talipes), or dislocation of the hips. Mental retardation is likely with severe associated hydrocephalus. Otherwise, the normal range of intelligence may be expected. Generally speaking, the higher up the spine the lesion, the greater the disability due to disruption of nervous tissue.

The treatment of spina bifida is a matter of some debate. Early surgery to remove the lump and cover the spinal cord is strongly argued by some medical experts, even though in spite of surgery, hydrocephalus, paralysis and incontinence in varying degrees may develop later. Psychologically, the mother is helped to feel that something is being done for her baby, whose initial appearance has been so distressing to her. Surgery also minimises the risk of other infections, as there is less of the damaged area exposed, and facilitates treatment for the accompanying conditions. Some arguments, however, have been put forward recommending no treatment, in the hope that the baby will die. Approximately 30 per cent of babies with spina bifida survive even without treatment, and deciding whether or not to operate immediately after birth is extremely difficult for both doctor and parents concerned. Assuming that treatment is provided, the surgical removal of the lump is the first priority, and, thereafter, treatment for hydrocephalus described above and for paralysis and incontinence.

The degree of damage to the spinal cord in spina bifida will affect the amount of weakness and paralysis of the legs. If the defect is at the base of the spine, the muscles of the feet and ankles may be the only ones affected and the child may have to wear short leg braces to help him walk. If the defect is in the middle of the thorax, the child may require a wheelchair as there will be flaccid paralysis below the waist. Physiotherapy to aid walking and to ensure that the limbs are kept in a normal position are part of the treatment. As there is sensory loss in the limbs, checking for bruises and sores that cannot be felt prevents the occurrence of ulcers which may become difficult to treat, leading in extreme instances to amputation.

The problem of incontinence of the bladder and bowel can be dealt with by bowel 'washouts' or manual expression of the bladder to keep the child clean and dry, and surgical procedures may also be undertaken by the urologist. Urinary infection and damage to the kidneys may cause serious complications.

The management of the child with spina bifida, both at home in the early years and eventually at school, can be complicated by the wide range of handicaps accompanying the condition. Much of the first part of a child's life is spent in hospital, and normal development is consequently disrupted. The psychological problems of incontinence are also difficult for a child to overcome, particularly when he ventures into normal social life. Incontinence is the biggest obstacle to a child's existence in a regular classroom. Even in special schools, a considerable amount of schooling is missed while a child is awaiting clean clothing, perhaps management and care. Special educational provision is probably necessary for approximately 66 per cent of the children, and approximately 25 per cent have no physical or intellectual problems; the remainder are severely intellectually handicapped.

Muscular Dystrophy

This condition is one of the myopathies in which there is a progressive weakening of the muscles. The muscle fibres swell, undergo what is known as 'hyeline degeneration' and become replaced by connective tissue and fat. These take up more space than the muscle they replace and the impression is given that the limbs have enlarged, hence the term 'pseudohypertrophy'.

The condition is caused by a recessive gene, and in its most severe form (duchenne type) affects young children, and boys in particular. There are different forms of the disease which vary considerably in their age of onset, rate of progress and mode of inheritance. However, there are certain symptoms common to all varieties when the condition begins in the muscles of the pelvic girdle, buttocks and thighs. These include slowness in walking, an inability to run and difficulty in rising from a fall. When the disease is established, a characteristic way of rising from the floor is for the child to turn on to his face, put his hands and feet on to the ground, and then climb his hands up his legs until he is upright. The early presentation of the disease gives the child a waddling or clumsy gait, often attributed to his being 'knock-kneed', lazy or flatfooted. His shoulders usually slope, and he has difficulty in raising objects or lifting his hands above his head. The form of the disease affecting the facial muscles leads to difficulty in closing the eyes or the lips tightly, and difficulty in whistling or blowing out the cheeks.

Pseudohypertrophic muscular dystrophy (duchenne type) usually begins at two or three years and renders the child incapable of walking by about ten or eleven. Muscular weakness and wasting of the muscles occur in the pelvic girdle, the thighs, the shoulder girdle and the upper arm. The pseudohypertrophy (enlargement of the muscles) is most apparent in the thighs and calves. Eventually the child becomes severely crippled and is unable to move the muscles of his body, except to be able to swallow and breathe. Death follows between the ages of fourteen and twenty, either from pneumonia or cardiac arrest, though some patients survive for longer in a severely crippled condition.

Limb girdle muscular dystrophy affects both sexes in equal numbers, beginning in the pelvic or shoulder girdle or both, where it may remain for several years before spreading to the other muscles. The condition may start in the second decade of life or even in some cases in middle or late life. Eventually a wheel-chair existence follows and the patient usually dies prematurely from some kind of respiratory infection. This form of the disease appears in the children of two unaffected carriers of the recessive gene.

Facioscapulohumeral muscular dystrophy also occurs in both sexes in equal numbers, usually in the second decade of life. The muscles of the face and the shoulder girdle are affected, the face assuming the expression of a mask. The patient has difficulties in closing the eyes and blowing out the cheeks as mentioned earlier. The disease, however, progresses very slowly and the disability is comparatively slight, so that most patients do not have a foreshortened life as a result of it. The probability of the condition being inherited from an affected individual is one in two.

These are the main varieties of the disease, though there are other extremely rare versions, and a condition known as dystrophia myotonia, which is not, strictly speaking, muscular dystrophy.

There is no drug yet able to cure the disease of muscular dystrophy. The management of the child with this condition is usually directed at activity rather than passivity. Children kept in bed invariably deteriorate, and gaining weight can also be a problem. Stretching the tendons, which are likely to shorten, helps to prevent contractures occurring, and a general attitude of optimism surrounding the child can counteract the depression which often builds up as the disease takes hold. Most school activities are within a child's capability in the early stages of the disease.

Scoliosis

This condition, a lateral curvature of the spine, is more common in girls than boys. One shoulder blade is more prominent than the other and one shoulder or hip higher than the other. There is no pain with the disorder. The cause is not known, though in some cases where there is a congenital abnormality of the vertebrae this may lead to the development of scoliosis. Polio may also cause curvatures, since the weakening of the muscles supporting the spine results in poor support of the bony vertebral column.

Treatment for this condition depends upon the extent of the curvature, its location, and the age of the child. An X-ray is taken of the entire spine and only if it deviates by more than 20 per cent from the normal is correction required. Surgery is performed in more serious cases. A brace may be used to control the scoliosis to straighten the spinal column, after which the child has to wear a plaster body jacket for six months and remain in bed for the whole period, although currently there are attempts to get the child up while still in the plaster cast, two or three weeks after surgery.

Cystic Fibrosis

This relatively common disease was only fully recognised in 1938 and
was thought to affect the pancreas. Later, however, it was thought to be
a generalised disease of mucus glands whose viscid mucus caused blockage and dilation of the glands. The disorder is now described as 'a
generalised disease affecting the exocrine glands' (Jolly, 1968). The
mucus glands distend, leading to dilation and consequent obstruction
and subsequent obstruction and fibrosis. The pancreas shrinks and is
replaced by fibrous tissue. Obstruction in the mucus glands of the
lungs causes bronchiectasis or emphysema, from which secondary
infection such as bronchopneumonia and lung abscesses usually follow.

The cause of cystic fibrosis is a recessive gene mutation. If a child
inherits the recessive gene from one parent he will become a carrrier.
Should he inherit from both, he will have the condition. Until recently,
many children having cystic fibrosis died in the first year of life from
pneumonia. Now, however, survival into adolescence and even adulthood is not uncommon. The first sign of the condition in the young
baby is failure to thrive or the failure to pass meconium in the neonatal
period. As the child grows, other symptoms of the disease appear,
including a persistent cough as the thick mucus builds up, offensive
stools, difficulty in breathing due to infections which gradually
damage the lungs,and clubbing of the fingers and toes after about
four or five years.

Once the condition is diagnosed, treatment consists of attention to
diet, which must have a high calorie content and protein, together with
restricted fat and starch, and the prevention and control of lung infection,
which, apart from antibiotics, includes breathing and coughing exercises, postural drainage and physiotherapy to keep the air passages
clear. The restrictions imposed on the child to prevent the spread of
infection may mean considerable isolation at home or in hospital. The
demands on the family and the need for medication and special diet at
school, together with uncertainty about the prognosis for a child with
this disease make it a very difficult situation for the adults and the
child concerned. As yet there is no known cure, but attempts at early
screening for the disease have been made.

Thalidomide

The availability of the drug thalidomide as a sedative for pregnant
women led, in 1958, to the birth of children with malformation of the

limbs as well as hearing defects. It is believed that intelligence was unaffected by the drug. The management of these children varies according to the nature and extent of the malformation due to arrested development of different parts of the embryo according to the stage at which the drug was administered. Help with toileting and feeding, the fitting of artificial limbs to an available joint where possible and the provision of wheel chairs may, as a result, mean comparatively little disruption to normal school and home life. Children with the additional handicaps of impaired vision or blindness, impaired hearing, facial paralysis, heart lesions or an impaired sense of balance require more specialised care, and will probably need special education.

Haemophilia

This is a disease arising from a sex-linked recessive gene mutation, transmitted by females but apparent only in males. The defect is an absence or deficiency of the anti-haemophilic factor, that is, the substance which causes blood to clot. The blood of the haemophiliac may take several hours or days to clot, the result being bleeding, both internal and external, into the joints, muscles' soft tissues and internal organs. Haemorrhages are also a severe problem. The result of repeated haemorrhages into the joints, particularly the knees, is limitation of movement and permanent crippling.

The condition usually comes to light in early childhood when prolonged bleeding follows a minor operation. Subsequently, the condition tends to improve, possibly because of greater care taken to avoid any accident to the body. Periods of ill health and confinement to bed as a result of bleeding can result in arrested growth.

Treatment and management of the disease include every precaution to ensure the safety of the growing child. This may involve wearing protective clothing at all times, and special care during any dental and surgical treatment. The specific treatment to stop bleeding is the intravenous administration of antihaemophilic globulin, which is prepared from human or animal sources. This is in very short supply, and as an alternative, fresh-frozen plasma is supplied.

Haemophiliac children are of normal intelligence, and unless the condition is very severe, they can attend ordinary school, provided that staff know what to do in the case of injury, and that adequate precautions are taken in sport and casual play. There may be much absence from school due to injury, but facilities for home study can remedy this. Schools for the physically handicapped do not necessarily provide the right education for these children, whose special medical needs and normal intellectual development present an awkward combination for a school to cope with satisfactorily. Many parents of such children feel dissatisfied with the current provision. The strain in terms of management of these children is great for both the child and the family.

Poliomyelitis

Advances in medical treatment and the provision of vaccine for immunisation for young babies against this infection have now brought under control what was once a disabling disease. The virus is spread by droplet infection and faecal contamination. The virus enters the blood stream and reaches the central nervous system, although it may be arrested at any stage of this process. Jolly (ibid.) defines four phases of the infection:

1. Silent infection, when the disease is in the alimentary tract;
2. Abortive poliomyelitis, when the virus is in both the alimentary and viraemic phases, the effect being an influenza-like illness;
3. Non-paralytic poliomyelitis, when the virus is in the alimentary, viraemic and neural phase, and an illness characterised by meningeal irritation is present;
4. Paralytic poliomyelitis, when the virus is in all three phases and its action on the neurone causes paralysis of the spinal cord, as well as other areas (bulbar poliomyelitis, polioencephalitis).

Treatment for the disease includes bed rest in isolation, the relief of pain by drugs, the use of splints to support joints and prevent deformities, respirator treatment for those whose muscles for breathing are affected, and after the acute phase of the infection has passed, active exercise and physiotherapy to build up muscle strength.

Heart Disease

Heart disease can be congenital or acquired, and children may be born with heart abnormalities. The number of children reaching school age with heart disease or congenital abnormalities is small and the causes are wide-ranging so it is not intended that much space be devoted to the subject here.

Rheumatic fever, with its associated effect on the functioning of the heart, is now comparatively rare in Western countries; so, too, is chorea (St Vitus's Dance), also associated with rheumatic fever. Pericarditis is found in a small proportion of children with juvenile rheumatoid arthritis (Still's disease – q.v.).

A few pupils with heart disease are to be found in schools for the physically handicapped. In general, they present similar educational and emotional problems to other children with chronic illness.

Asthma

'Asthma' means 'breathing hard' but there is no generally agreed medical definition of the word. Here it is defined as 'a clinical disorder characterized by intermittent bronchospasm with symptom-free intervals. Its main symptoms are wheeze, shortness of breath, cough and sometimes tenacious sputum' (Simpson, 1973).

Asthma can be classified into allergic and non-allergic types. The allergic patient often has a family history of allergic disorders such as hay fever and a personal history of eczema. The non-allergic patient has symptoms more likely to be provoked by bacterial infection or emotional stimuli. There is considerable overlap between the two types. Infection usually comes from the upper respiratory tract, though it can be provoked by any viral infection. The emotional factor can frequently be seen in the personality of children with asthma who are often nervous, sensitive and sometimes disturbed. In the Isle of Wight study of 9-, 10- and 11-year-old children, 10.5 per cent of children with asthma had 'concomitant psychiatric disorder'. Frequently, the cause of emotional stress is in the home and many asthmatic patients cease to have attacks on removal to boarding school.

Asthmatic Attack

The attack comes on suddenly, bronchospasm causing respiratory obstruction with greater difficulty in expiration than inspiration. In some children the onset of an attack is heralded by a running nose due to allergic rhinitis, which is often described as 'a cold'. This differs from the common cold in that the nasal discharge is persistently clear. [A cough is another symptom preceding an attack.] In a severe attack the child becomes cyanosed [turns blue] and very frightened, thereby causing a vicious circle of increasing respiratory distress. . . Bronchospasm usually stops suddenly but the attack itself tails off rather than has a sudden end. One reason'for this is that secretions become retained in the narrowed bronchi and must be coughed away before the lungs are clear. These accumulated secretions cause an alteration in the adventitious sounds from the chest which commence with an audible wheeze and change to a rattle. (Jolly, 1968).

Most children with asthma are of normal physical appearance but some have so-called 'adenoidal facies' [*sic*] with narrow maxilla, high palate and malocclusion. Children with chronic asthma tend to be slender and slightly below average in weight. Some develop barrel-shaped chests.

Treatment of an acute attack consists of physiotherapy and anti-spasmodic drugs.

Status Asthmaticus

This term is generally used to denote a prolonged attack and a recognition of a life-threatening situation and the urgent need to provide adequate therapeutic measures (Simpson, 1973).

Prevalence

'It has been estimated that about 150,000 children in England and Wales have asthma for a longer or shorter period during their school life. More school days are lost on account of asthma than any other condition, and for years it has been the most frequent condition giving rise to admission to special schools for delicate children' (Simpson, 1973).

Although asthma has a low death rate the number of deaths directly attributable to asthma has grown in recent years: 30 in the 5 to 14 age group in 1961 to 98 in 1967, in England and Wales. In 1968 the number dropped to 57.

Long-term Treatment

Treatment may include environmental controls (i.e. removing sources of allergens in the child's environment), hyposensitisation (attempting to build up resistance to allergens), physiotherapy and breathing exercises, use of drugs to relieve symptoms and measures to lessen emotional and psychological disturbances, possibly involving the help of a child psychiatrist. It is essential that the parents of an asthmatic patient are fully involved in the various aspects of long-term management and have all the measures properly explained to them.

Educational

The greatest problem of educational progress for an asthmatic child is missed schooling. In addition, there may be anxiety at apparent failure at school. The emotional problems described above may be reflected in behaviour in the classroom. For teachers, a point worth noting is that in the period immediately before an asthmatic attack, when the child is showing preliminary symptoms, possibly unrecognised by the teacher, the child will probably not be 'taking in' what the teacher is saying. It is worthwhile, therefore, repeating that part of the lesson to the child later, when he has fully recovered from the attack.

Arthritis in Children: Juvenile Rheumatoid arthritis: Still's Disease

The cause of arthritis in children is unkown. It is chronic and can have recurrent 'flare-ups'. According to a local study its prevalence is estimated at 0.65 per cent or one case per 1500 of the school population (Bywaters, 1966). Girls are affected more than boys.

Arthritis in children used, in Britain, to be called Still's disease, a term covering the disease generally. This was after Frederic Still, who first recognised certain special features of this childhood disease, which include a characteristic rash, high fever, enlargement of spleen and liver as well as joint involvement. Elsewhere the disease was called juvenile rheumatoid arthritis. Recent research has revealed numerous different patterns of arthritis disease in children. Nevertheless, in all patterns of the disease the joints are affected as in rheumatoid arthritis.

Between the bones of hinged joints (e.g. elbow and knee) and sliding joint (vertebrae) will be found cartilage covered by a greasy 'skin' called a synovial membrane. In the ball and socket joint (e.g. shoulder and hips) the synovial membrane forms a bag or capsule between the bones which becomes filled with an oily fluid, given out by the membrane, called the synovial fluid. In arthritis, the synovial membrane becomes inflamed and secretes extra synovial fluid which begins to attack the cartilage. The joint becomes inflamed and swollen. Eventually the bones become demineralised at the ends (osteoporosis). This can be followed by periostitis (inflammation of the periosteum) in the region of the inflamed joint. In extreme cases, the bone ends fuse and become ankylosed (joined together) with the destruction of the cartilage. However, the process can stop at any time.

A few children, mostly girls, have a pattern of illness similar to that of adult rheumatoid arthritis. Although the age of onset can be as early as five years, usually it is at twelve years or later. This form often starts with involvement of small joints and spreads to other joints. The activity of the disease is persistent and can continue intermittently for years. Strong drugs, such as penicillamine are used as quickly as possible to halt the activity of the disease.

Another form of the disease, mostly affecting boys, is a form of spinal arthritis — ankylosing spondylitis. The age of onset is usually nine to twelve years, although it can be much earlier. These children tend to carry HLA27, an inherited antigen which can be identified by tissue typing. This helps in the early recognition of the disease (Ansell, 1976).

Some children have a systemic form of the disease. Others have the disease in several joints (poliarthritis) and some have it involving a few joints (pauciarticular). It is in the pauciarticular group that eye involvement is often found. It used to be the case that children occasionally lost their sight becaue of inflammation of the eye but nowadays, by early detection, drugs and surgery, this is less likely.

Treatment of arthritis in children consists of drug therapy and hydrotherapy. Occasionally, surgery is used to correct a deformity or replace a joint. Measures to relieve pain and relax muscles and joints include wax treatment, 'hot packs' and use of the Faradic footbath (a footbath at the bottom of which are electric plates through which a current is passed).

Effects of Arthritis in Children

Growth is affected by arthritis in children, causing children to be stunted and/or possibly causing anomalies of growth, e.g. one leg longer than the other. It is also a very painful disease, often necessitating strong dosage of drugs, with the consequent side-effects. The chronic nature of the disease with the intermittent 'flare-ups' frequently causes poor school attendance.

SECTION 2 : PSYCHOLOGICAL ISSUES

The aim of this section is to relate recent medical, biochemical and psychological research to different areas of learning and to draw attention to the relevance and implications of this research to motor and neurological impairment in children.

3 LEARNING AND DISORDERS OF PERCEPTION

Intellectual abilities and their development are influenced by cerebral organisation, which includes the central nervous system. A knowledge of the functioning of a healthy brain system is necessary, therefore, if one is to understand the process of learning and the way difficulties in learning arise if the brain is damaged. The unlocking of the secrets of the brain and an understanding of the working of the nervous system seem possible in the next few decades — advances made possible only as a result of work, begun many years ago, by scientists of various disciplines.

In the absence of techniques for measuring or observing brain function directly, early scientists and theorists conceived the notion of 'intelligence', the manifestation of brain performance, and it has been recognised since the mid-nineteenth century that a healthy, well-formed brain is a necessary requirement for intelligence to be developed and sustained. Charles Darwin was one of the earliest scientists to recognise a progression from animal to human mental function. Later, the neurologist Lloyd Morgan (1894) offered a more technical view of this development. In 1870 Herbert Spencer advanced a sophisticated theory that recent and complex mental capacities evolved from the foundation laid down by older and simpler mechanisms paralleling the organisation of the nervous system. Darwin's writings clearly influenced Spencer's ideas which in turn influenced Spearman (1927), whose work on the nature of intelligence is best known for his theory that all intellectual performance is hierarchically organised and is influenced by general ability, or 'g'. Alfred Binet (1896) contributed much to our understanding of the nature of intelligence. He sought a direct measure of intelligence by observing an individual's performance in a range of activities such as attention, motor skill, comprehension, language ability and memorising. There had been earlier attempts to give a systematic account of the relationship between the structure of the nervous system and specific functions — in 1824 Flourens had perceived the division of the nervous system into its six principal assemblies: the cerebral hemispheres, the cerebellum, the medulla oblongata, the corpora quadrigemina, the spinal cord and the peripheral nerves. His argument was that all these units acted in concert, and he resisted attempts to relate specific mental functions — perception, memory, judgement — to areas within the cerebral hemisphere.

Hughlings Jackson (1874) developed Flouren's ideas and was more willing to link mental activities to hierarchical levels of nervous functioning, though Jackson too remained hesitant about identifying specific cerebral structures with higher functioning such as judgement and memory. However, the arguments for localisation of function within the cortex were becoming more convincing. As early as 1870 Fritsch and Hitzig showed that stimulation of certain areas of the cerebral cortex by a galvanic current evoked motor responses. Later, in 1876, Ferrier demonstrated that vision was localised in the occipital cortex. Other functions such as hearing, speech and comprehension had been traced to the temporal lobes by Broca, Wernicke and others (for a fuller account see Penfield and Roberts, 1959). Now began the era of the 'map makers' which led to some excessive zeal and optimism about the location of 'centers' for higher cognitive functioning within the cerebral hemispheres.

Lashley's meticulous work, spanning forty years up to 1929, in search of the memory trace (engram) suggested that learning was dependent on the integrity and total mass action of the cerebral regions (equipotentiality) rather than on localised centres. He recognised, however, that specialised cerebral areas were responsible for certain sensory and motor functions. Lashley's views lent much support to the unitary character of intelligence 'g', but Lashley also believed the 'correlated development of different cerebral areas sustaining distinct functions was an equally tenable hypothesis'.

Intelligence

Interest now shifted to the development of intelligence in the individual. The British school of thought first propounded by Sir Cyril Burt (1940, 1955) was that intellectual development follows neurological maturation within the central nervous system and is hierarchically organised.

Since the 1940s Hebb has exerted a powerful influence on ideas about the development of intelligence and cerebral organisation. Hebb rejected Lashley's notion of mass action, demonstrating that the effects of massive cerebral lesions on intellectual function in adults was less severe than in children. A young child's language skills, for example, were more vulnerable to impairment than that of an adult who suffered a similar lesion provided it did not affect 'certain crucial areas'. This demonstrates that particular skills cannot develop if certain areas of the brain are damaged. An adult has already acquired the skill. If the whole brain were responsible for mental activity, child and adult would be equally affected.

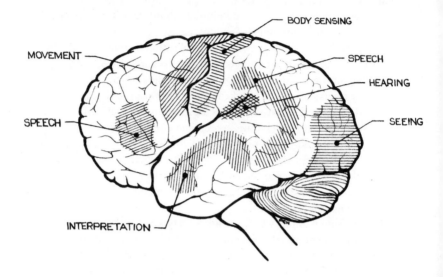

Figure 2.   Brain Structure Showing Areas in Cerebral Hemispheres
Associated with Cognitive Functioning

Hebb's theory of two types of intelligence — intelligence A and intelligence B — is based on a neurological foundation.   Intelligence A is
commonly used to denote the 'capacity for development, a fully innate
potential that amounts to the possession of a good brain and a good
natural "metabolism".   However, Hebb maintains that the level of
efficiency will depend upon the environmental influences; and this level
can be directly measured — intelligence B. Hebb proposes that once
intelligence B is established, it no longer needs the full powers of a good
brain to be serviced and is only peripherally affected by brain injury
or degeneration. Hebb stresses the dependence of the infant brain
for intellectual performance on the hierarchical organisation of
intellectual skills. He insists that systematic and repeated experiences
for young children are a prerequisite for developing intellectual skills.
This theory has a neurological basis. Learning is facilitated by neurological changes which Hebb describes as cell assemblies and elaborations of
cell assemblies leading to 'phase sequences'.

Piaget's view of intelligence is also hierarchical. He regards intelligence as biological adaptation and its evolution as a result of human physical encounters with the environment. In a sense it parallels Hebb's neurological descriptions of levels of nervous system organisation. Piaget's ontogenetic formulations about invariant stages of development increasing in complexity at each stage are not unlike Hebb's neurophysiological propositions about the nature of intelligence.

The important effects of cerebral lesions on intellectual development at particular ontogenetic stages become clear. The size, location and timing of cerebral insult would influence the level of cognitive functioning. Recent studies have revealed sex differences in the development of cerebral function and there has been a return to the search for localisation.

Sex Differences

There is evidence that certain abilities and traits are unevenly distributed between males and females. (For a fuller discussion see Buffery and Gray, 1972). Consistent differences are shown in verbal and spatial skills. It is hypothesised that the female's greater facility in handling words and the male's superiority in performing tasks demanding perception, judgement and manipulation of spatial relationships are due to differences in the development and structure of male and female brains. It is known, for instance, that girls' brains develop more rapidly than boys'. This is particularly true of the cerebellum which develops faster in females up to the age of three years. By six months the cerebellum weight in girls is twice as great as that in boys. It is this pattern of difference in growth and ability between the sexes (rather than psycho-social influences) that accounts for differential superiority in language, science and mathematics. There is some evidence to suggest that these differences persist until adulthood (Buffery, 1971).

Asymmetries of Structures and Functions

The brain receives verbal and spatial information and these stimuli are delivered in the form of codes. Verbal information such as speech, seeking interpretation in the brain, is sequentially delivered — that is, it follows an order — whereas spatial information is rendered in simultaneous code — input and output overlaps. It is hypothesised that verbal information (sequential codes) is best served by neural structures of the brain which are adjacent and are localised and are predominantly lateralised to the left cerebral hemisphere. Such a topographic structure, it is argued, becomes 'specialised for the extraction of linguistic features in speech perception' and the development of verbal functions and language. It is further argued that localisation has advantages because it can organise and handle information efficiently, and avoid messages being wasted by unnecessary involvement of mass neuronal activity. On the other hand, simultaneous coding is diffusely represented in the brain because general spatial skills of crawling, walking, reaching and eye-hand co-ordination demand the co-ordination of input into the brain from eyes, ears and limbs and could not be efficiently handled by localised areas of the brain. What is well established is that language skills are organised in the left hemisphere but spatial skills are not absolutely biased, but well presented to the right. . .

Buffery (1970) suggests that there is some special structural attraction which invites the left cerebral hemisphere to serve the sequential coding — 'an innate, species specific neural mechanism which is usually lateralised to and localised within whichever cerebral hemisphere of the human brain is to develop dominance for language function'. It will be remembered that the right hemisphere controls physical action on the left side of the body and vice versa. Gazzaniga and Sperry (1967), however, have pointed out that even for right-handers (who normally have left-hemisphere dominance for language) language is not absolutely established in the left hemisphere. The right hemisphere does possess rudimentary verbal organisational facility.

Psychological tests of vision and hearing have revealed differences in function between right and left hemispheres. In the right field of vision, which is organised by the left hemisphere, superiority has been found for perceiving alphabetical material and familiar objects. The left field, controlled by the right hemisphere, has been found superior for face recognition and location and for perceiving quantities of dots. In dichotic listening (simultaneous auditory stimulation of ears) the right ear has been found superior for discriminating digits, words and consonants. The left ear has advantage for non-verbal sounds such as melodies and simple pitch. In other words there is right hemisphere specialisation for discrimination of non-verbal sounds. Clinical support for this is to be found in cases of patients with right anterior temporal lobectomy (Milner, 1971).

There are anatomical asymmetries in the cerebral structures, the left cerebral hemisphere being slightly heavier, occupying more space and having higher specific gravity than the right. Buffery and Gray proposed that the human neuronal or foetal female brain might reveal 'pre-language' structural asymmetry: this is supported by data (Wada, 1969 ; Witelson and Pallie, 1973) which confirmed functional precocity and greater myelination in *female* non-brain-injured babies that had been aborted or who had died perinatally.

Neuroscientific Contributions

A new understanding of the human brain springs from the work of James Watson and Francis Crick who, in 1953, revealed the structure of the DNA (deoxyribonucleic acid) molecule. Their discovery that DNA is the significant substance by which hereditary information is coded has given us a clearer idea of the way in which characteristics of one generation are handed down to another.

Watson and Crick indicated how the long strings of DNA, strands which are two complementary helical (spiral) strands, are assembled. The process originates when one strand of the DNA double helix unwinds. Each single old strand forms into a new double helix, and the process of replication continues. Precise rules dictate the way 'bases' (organic substances adenine, cytosine, thymine and guanine) are paired. Bonding of the double helix is achieved by adherence to strict chemical sequencing and combination of each pair (adenine to thymine, and cytosine to guanine alone) to ensure genetic stability or continuity.

Biological information is stored in DNA. One of the functions of DNA is to replicate itself. The other purpose is to ensure that living cells receive the necessary information for the manufacture of compounds. Genetic information is transferred from DNA to RNA (ribonucleic acid, found in the cell itself) according to equally strict rules governing DNA duplication. This is accomplished by the synthesis of DNA and RNA into amino acids (organic compounds containing nitrogen) which eventually combine to form proteins (larger molecules consisting of combinations of amino acids) to undertake the biological functions dictated by the gene. The gene in the DNA provides the necessary code for a specific protein.

A controversial suggestion has been advanced that scientists might intervene directly in the genetic process to correct hereditary anomalies, occasioned by sudden and persistent DNA changes, or when base and amino acid variations occur. Some outcomes of such mutations in man are genetic diseases such as haemophilia (a sex-linked inheritance), phenylketonuria(PKU), a recessive gene, Down's syndrome (presence of an extra chromosome) and hereditary changes resulting in sickle cell anaemia. The long-term hope is that it might be possible to correct DNA errors — first, by prompt recognition of mistakes and, second, by the speedy restoration of the orderly processes of replication and genetic stability.

The Chemistry of Learning and Memory

A recent hypothesis is that the DNA code is implicated directly or indirectly in learning, memory and other processes. Memory, for example, is possibly coded into long chains of molecules. The theory is that consolidation and maintenance of memory is dependent upon the production of particular proteins.

In theory this is possible. A group of scientists at Oxford, who have been experimenting with tissue cultures, have succeeded in implanting the nucleus of a cell from the intestine of a donor tadpole into an unfertilised egg cell of a tadpole of the same species; the nucleus of the recipient egg cell had been previously destroyed by ultra violet light. The frog's egg, equipped with its full complement of chromosomes, instead of only the half set, began to divide and behaved as if it was fertilised conventionally. Finally, it grew into a tadpole. Whether we can engage in bolder endeavours to control the effects of 'failures' in genetic mechanism is a question of whether we can overcome enormous technical problems and considerable ethical anxieties. In the future it might be possible to destroy the faulty parts of the nucleus and replace them.

Watson and Crick are the direct inheritors of the knowledge amassed by a distinguished and energetic line of molecular biologists, geneticists, biochemists and neuroscientists. The most recent work of the biochemists has contributed to our knowledge of mental processes by examining chemical substances which seem to be intimately associated with the transmission of neural impulses. Sir John Eccles and his colleagues at the Australian National University of Canberra, using the electron microscope and sophisticated micro-electrode techniques for probing single nerve cells, identified acetylcholine as one of these specialised compounds.

Learning and memory are two processes that are reported to be singularly susceptible to chemical agents in the brain. Sperry's (1963) work with goldfish, in which he cut the optic nerve fibres and observed their mode of regeneration (a feature of lowly vertebrates, amphibians and fish only) and the accuracy with which the nerve fibres of the right eye sought out the left side of the brain and vice versa, led him to speculate that an electro-chemical basis for neural precision exists. Sperry believes that the rich exchange of signals, whereby cells recognise one another, is chemically facilitated.

The most exciting development, however, in this field was led by the brilliant Swedish neurobiologist Holger Hyden (1958), working at the

University of Goteborg. Hyden, using sophisticated microknives and minute wire instruments to remove the smaller glial cells (glue-like structures or tissue) that surround the neuron, analysed each component for its protein synthesis, RNA production and content and other biochemical ingredients. He noted that rabbits and rats, for example, who 'learned' new tasks showed *an increase in RNA synthesis* and also that various stages of learning were related to levels of *RNA activity*. New stimuli result in small additional changes in the RNA synthesis and sensory impulses trigger off activities in neural DNA.

These and other experiments led to a number of 'cannibal' experiments which attempted to transfer RNA molecules from trained animals to naive subjects. Untutored worms were fed with portions of others which had acquired skills such as shock avoidance and untrained rats were injected with brain extracts from trained rats. Attempts at replicating these memory transfer studies have been highly unsuccessful. Graver doubts may be expressed as to whether such a mode of transmission is possible in humans, as is claimed in the animal transfer experiments.

What is now known, however, is that the brain cortex of rats which 'learned' new skills weighed about 5 per cent more than their untrained litter mates, and that marked differences were noted in the neural enzyme activity and an increase in glial cells in experimental stimulated litter mates. Furthermore, small amounts of an antibiotic (puromycin), a substance known to block RNA-mediated protein synthesis, inhibits the formation of long-term memory of newly learned tasks. Flexner, Flexner and Stellar (1963) reported that mice taught to avoid electric shock forgot the habit when puromycin was injected into their brain. The period of memory loss was directly related to such factors as the interval between learned tasks (1–43 days) and the sites chosen (frontal, ventricular and temporal regions) for injecting puromycin. The findings strongly suggested that continued protein synthesis is necessary for the maintenance of memory. Memory processes of fish seemed less vulnerable to puromycin.

If we are to survive we need protection from the overwhelming stream of energy impinging upon us. The function of the brain and nervous system is to filter the mass of information competing for our attention. How its complex system protects us remains unclear. What is known is that when selective or gross damage to various structures of the brain occur through underdevelopment, disease or malformation, then brain working becomes disturbed and function impaired. The capacity of the individual to perceive, remember, plan actions, invent symbol systems and have access to other people's experience is marked-ly reduced. Neurophysiological psychologists have shown considerable interest in the effects of brain lesion upon function and various explanations or descriptions have been offered as to the qualitative and quantitative effects of brain injury upon psychological functioning. As has been shown, it is difficult to establish with certainty the precise relationship between anatomical structure and functioning. (There are a few exceptions: for example, form discrimination is located in the visual cortex but this function is not strictly limited to this site.) It would be unwise necessarily to relate weaknesses in function to the presence of lesions or to assume that specific learning difficulties in children must be attributed to neurological damage. The inadequacy of using cortical damage signs as predictors or explanations of disordered function has often been remarked (Herbert, 1964). It would clearly be very useful in planning instructional strategies if we had reliable knowledge of the extent to which healing and adaptation occurs, the manner in which intact areas take over from inactive regions, how a spontaneous recovery of function takes place and the effects of loss of neural facilitation on unaffected cortical or sub-cortical areas.

In Britain, Canada and elsewhere, it was not until World War Two that neurologists and psychologists came together to direct their interest and technology to study brain injury in humans. Two major issues emerged:

the need for more accurate descriptions of the major clinical conditions and of their aetiology;
descriptions of the intellectual characteristics of brain-injured subjects and their relationship to cerebral dysfunction.

Among the more commonly studied psychological processes have been disorders of perception:

visual-auditory
spatial and motor functioning.

(a) Visual Perception

Kinsbourne and Warrington (1962, 1963) suggested that the reason why four subjects who experienced difficulty with tasks involving visual recognition of pictures and extended scenes — 'simultanagnosia' — a specific disorder of form perception, was that they had suffered damage in the anterior portion of the left occipital lobe. These subjects could readily recognise single forms but more than one form only after prolonged exposure to the stimuli.

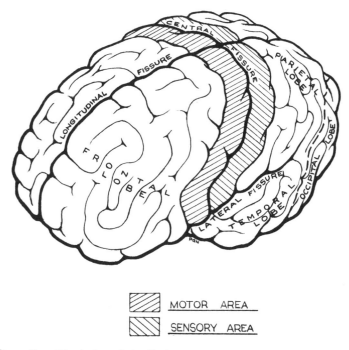

MOTOR AREA

SENSORY AREA

Figure 3.   The Lobes of the Brain

Milner (1958) demonstrated that removal of the right temporal lobe interfered with the ability to interpret pictorial material. Among other examples of visual perceptual defects provoked by specific neurological injury is that of size constancy judgements — consequent upon parietal lobe damage (Wyke, 1960). Persons with unilateral cortical lesions reveal impairments in face recognition and discrimination of shape and position of lines.

(b) Auditory Perception

There has been less research in auditory than in visual perception partly because of technical limitations. The effects of excision or disease to such areas as the auditory cortex in the left or right temporal lobes reveal differences in ability to discriminate pitch, volume, rhythm and ability to locate auditory stimuli (Milner, 1962).

(c) Spatial and Motor Functioning: Route-Finding Difficulty

A less frequently mentioned disability is one in which a person has difficulty in finding his way about familiar surroundings. Such a person is unable to relate himself to a fixed point in space. Poor navigational performance and disordered judgement of motion have been reported by Goody, Benton, Brain and others (Benton, 1969). Some research workers ascribe this weakness to an inability to focus attention adequately, while others (Brain, 1941) attribute this disorder to 'confusion and complexity' occasioned in the individual when apparently random responses are demanded at decision points. They show a tendency to make right turns at these points on a route, become perplexed and make capricious responses at choice points. This is highlighted in hemianopic (blind in one half of the visual field) patients.

It is further suggested that children with movement disorders, who have proprioceptive and tactile weaknesses, experience difficulties in navigating in single, double or three directions (left to right or vice versa, up/down, side/side). Since spatial orientation has a neurological basis, this faculty becomes affected in persons with specific neuro-logical lesions (Goody, 1969).

(d) Disorders of Execution (Dyspraxias)

Studies of disorientation of space and time in subjects with lesions to such cortical areas as the angular, supramarginal gyri, adjacent occipital, parietal and temporal regions have been received by Benton (1969).

Subjects show difficulties in reading, apprehending more than four digits and in copying complex figures. They also show marked inability in finding their way about familiar surroundings. Such impairments in visual localisation and spatial orientation are not necessarily influenced by occulomotor, central or visual field defects in patients. For instance, some subjects with impaired visual acuity do not in fact reveal con-comitant weaknesses in spatial orientation, whilst others with defective ability to localise stimuli in space do not have visual field disturbances.

Others with short-term memory defects for spatial location (e.g. in an alternative choice test fail to match complex figures when the model is removed) have been found to have lesions in the occipital or right parietal regions.

(e) Visuo-Constructive Weaknesses

The disorder may show up in such tasks as an inability to build a tower of bricks, to construct a six-cube pyramid, or to copy a shape or pattern with sticks or plasticine. A child who is required to place one brick upon another must not only possess a degree of manual dexterity and eye-hand co-ordination, but be aware of the orientation of such objects in space and engage in an analysis of their interrelations — thus efficient muscular organisation and adequate spatial judgements are needed at the simplest level of visuo-constructive tasks. The essence of visuo-constructive weakness lies in being unable to translate adequate visual perception into appropriate visuo-motor actions.

Abercrombie (1964) has reviewed the literature concerning these disorders in brain-injured children including CP subjects. Wedell (1973), in his account of learning and perceptuo-motor disabilities, warns against accepting general statements about the 'relationship between CNS defects and disabilities in sensory motor organization', since the findings of the studies are highly equivocal.

Asymmetry of Cortical Functions

Warrington (1969) has argued that anatomical support for the view of asymmetry of cortical functions is strong. Lesions to the right hemisphere tend to cause disorders of constructional ability and weakness in 'incorporating information into the constructional task'. It is claimed that errors of proportion and spatial relationships result from damage to the right hemisphere. Conversely, lesions to the left hemisphere lead to a heterogeneous group of disorders in planning and carrying out the motor component of a task.

Learning in Children with Neurological and Motor Disabilities

By virtue of his motor disorder, the child with neurological and motor disabilities faces a number of formidable difficulties over a whole range of learning tasks. The CP child, for instance, is restricted in his ability to move about freely in space and there are indications of the possible adverse effects of this on the child's ability to handle perceptuo-motor information. There is reason to suspect that in such children, judgements of space and orientation, crucial to the development of such personal social skills as dressing, feeding, toileting and playing are affected, especially if the children are raised in an impoverished social and physical environment. A number of studies have indicated that speech and language of such children develop more slowly than in normal children (Jones *et al.*, 1969). When a child is faced with a dual handicap of motor and verbal limitation, he is unable to relate language to practical experiences and the stream of discourse, such as 'eat your

apple', 'give me the red pencil', and 'get into your bath', becomes a
string of inconsequential sounds, if he is unable to carry out the appropriate physical actions consequent upon verbal instructions.

The failure to acquire the necessary skills leads to further intellectual
loss, characterised by a slowness to respond to complex environmental
demands. If one of the distinguishing aspects in humans is the rate at
which they process information, then their slowness to adapt in a learning situation, in the classroom or home, would be their chief characteristic.

It can be argued that neurologically impaired children are slower
('less intelligent') because they do not employ an appropriate strategy
when obliged to extract meaning from the ceaseless input of information from the environment. They are slow learners because they have
not learnt to focus attention on the relevant aspects of the stimuli, or
to withdraw attention from excessive information. These children
differ from fast learners not only in their capacity to learn, but their
approach to a learning situation.

Implications for Teachers

The implications for teachers have a direct relevance to classroom
instruction procedures. Teachers should guard against 'overloading' the
information, to use engineering terminology. Some of the other finer
points relate to memory and apprehension span, as children perform
best when information presented is controlled and issued in manageable
units (the optimum level for individual children should be determined
by the class teacher). Teachers should discourage guessing in children,
thereby reducing errors. Repetition and practice to consolidate previously learned material is strongly indicated and the risk of random learning
minimised by avoiding unnecessary alternative choices in learning tasks.
Other methods of structured planning of activity for the design and
content of material which should be presented to children are discussed
in subsequent chapters of the book.

4 BRAIN-DAMAGED CHILDREN

This chapter deals with the confusion surrounding the term 'brain-damaged child', a term which covers many different conditions. An account of learning disorders caused by brain damage follows, and some suggestions are made for their remediation.

Parents, neurologists, psychologists and educators are often confused about the meaning of the term 'brain-damaged child', which has become one of the diagnostic sub-categories to which children with a diversity of learning and behavioural problems have been assigned. In the current literature as many as forty different terms are used to refer to these children, but, the most commonly accepted meaning is that of a child with a minimal disturbance of cerebral function rather than one suffering from cerebral palsy, epilepsy or mental subnormality. To clarify the position for professionals and parents directly concerned with these children, the first part of this account will attempt to trace the ways in which the confused terminology arose and examine the intellectual and behavioural patterns it has come to imply. Ways in which the term may most usefully be re-defined will then be suggested. The second part of the account will deal specifically with the learning disorders associated with actual damage, particularly cerebral palsy.

In the 1920s a German neurologist, Dr Strauss, examined the children of a school for mental defectives in Michigan in the USA and found that a large proportion had some kind of neurological impairment. From these findings, Strauss postulated that mental defectives could not be considered as a homogeneous group, but rather that they consisted of an 'endogenous' and an 'exogenous' group. The endogenous group showed no history of perinatal or later childhood damage to the nervous system and their backwardness could be ascribed to an inherited low intelligence. The exogenous group showed actual damage to the central nervous system, or the brain. Collaborating with a psychologist, Dr Laura Lehtinen, Strauss drew attention to the fact that there were differences in both cognitive and emotional behaviour between the two groups and that the exogenous group showed specific learning difficulties and abnormal patterns of behaviour. For example, small demands or changes in the children's routine could result in an unpredictable show of temper. The term 'brain-damaged' subsequently came to be applied to the exogenous group.

The criteria Strauss used for the recognition of cases of brain injury were:

1. injury to the brain by trauma or inflammatory processes before, during, or after birth;
2. slight neurological signs indicating a lesion;
3. severe psychological disturbance together with intellectual retardation despite normal family stock;
4. no mental retardation but the presence of psychological disturbance discovered by means of qualitative tests of perception and conceptualisation.

Unfortunately, both exogenous and endogenous groups of children were found to conform to some of Strauss's criteria, although it is true that a child who shows these signs is more likely to be brain-damaged than one who does not. Difficulties still arise from the rather loose application of the term 'brain-damaged', since children have been found depicting one or more Strauss criteria but showing no clinical signs of brain damage. Others who are definitely known to be brain-damaged have been found to display none of these criteria.

Attempts to overcome the difficulty by using terms such as 'soft neurological signs', 'minimal cerebral dysfunction', 'diffuse' or 'non-focal' are again begging the question, since 'brain damage' is being implied. It has been pointed out (Birch, 1963) that a distinction should be made between the fact of brain damage and the concept of brain damage.

The fact of brain damage is the presence of any anatomical or physiological change of a pathological nature in the nerve tissues of the brain. Thus a child with cerebral palsy is, in fact, brain-damaged.

The extent of the functional disturbance resulting from brain damage will depend on a number of factors. These include:

1. size of the lesion;
2. site of the lesion;
3. whether the lesion is active or static;
4. whether it is diffuse or focal;
5. whether the damage occurred during the pre-natal or neonatal period. If there is an early primary lesion, there may be secondary consequences, since interrelated areas, dependent on the damaged area for stimulation towards maturation, may fail to develop.

The concept of brain damage, which is not necessarily applicable to all children with brain damage, is defined as applicable to the individual with damage to the nervous system, which may have resulted in some primary disorganisation. The individual could develop abnormal patterns of behaviour, with disturbed interpersonal and social features. For example, in a child's family relationships, his disturbances may affect parental attitudes and the child may be rejected because of behaviour he cannot control or understand. Such rejection could lead to further behavioural disturbance. Clearly such dysfunction may lead indirectly to impaired development of his self-image, since this is derived from the way others view him (with possible hostility or impatience) and from the way he sees himself (bad, stupid or doomed to failure). Unfortunately, these beliefs lead to unrealistic expectations to succeed

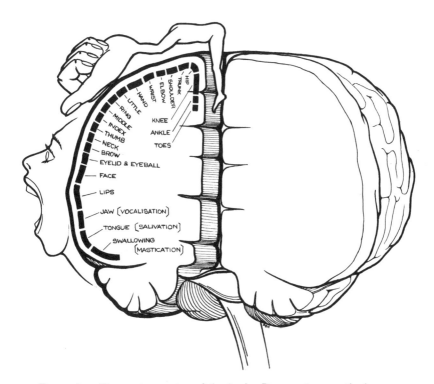

Figure 4.   The motor cortex of the brain. Damage to a particular section of the motor cortex results in physical impairment to the equivalent function.

or attempts to gain attention by clowning or aggressiveness. The concept usually refers to a certain pattern of behavioural disturbance, and
this stereotyping has meant the neglect of consideration of other
behaviour disorders in such children.

Disturbances in Spatial Perception

Strauss and Lehtinen believed that the behaviour of the children they
studied indicated perceptual disturbances which were in many ways
similar to those of brain-injured adults. For example, the children
would examine intently certain interesting details of the teacher's
clothing, such as belts or buckles and seemed oblivious of anything else;
or they might be attracted to the minute details of pictures but dis-
regard the conceptual contents of the picture as a whole. The children
experienced particular difficulty in writing and arithmetic and performed erratically and incorrectly on puzzles and performance tests.
In order to objectify these clinical impressions, various perceptual and
motor tests, such as the marble-board test were administered in which
brain-injured children showed a qualitatively different performance
from the familial mentally deficient child or younger normal child. The
results of the marble-board and other perceptual tests suggested that
brain-injured children had particular *figure-background* difficulties and
this hypothesis was supported by results of a test in which children had
to perceive embedded figures; the children experienced greater difficulty
than normal children in distinguishing foreground from background. It
was considered that the foreground/background disturbance might
apply to other modalities (i.e. to the tactual and auditory fields as well
as to the visual field) and results of a variety of tests suggested that this
was so. It appears that brain-damaged children experience constant
instability between foreground and background so that there is a fluid
and fluctuating background to the child's adjustment to the normal
world. This is obviously a handicap in all learning processes; in reading,
for example, children may be unable to attend to the essential word
(the 'figure') long enough to make an appropriate response. Since the
hundreds of other stimuli (pattern, spaces and angles) may distract
his attention, clearly there is a relationship between such difficulties
and the cognitive disorders which Strauss and Lehtinen drew particular
attention to, that is, the difficulties of these children in concept
formation and in forming abstractions. Obviously a child will have
difficulties in abstracting the class characteristics of a stimulus pattern
(and in reducing it to a standardised de-particularised problem) if he
cannot cut out its detailed particularities (e.g. size and colour). The

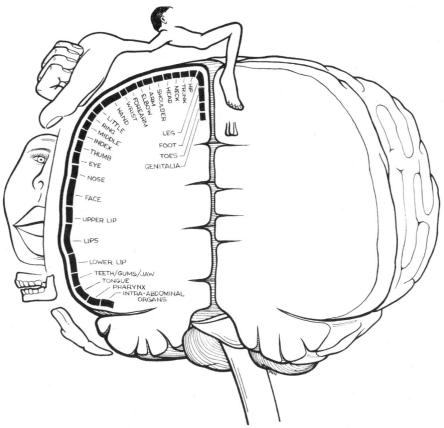

Figure 5. The sensory cortex of the brain. The localisation of each function corresponds with a particular section of the sensory cortex.

foreground/background confusion and the inability to see things as wholes may also be closely related to some of the behavioural disorders noted in brain-damaged children.

Behavioural Disorders: General Characteristics

Strauss and Lehtinen found behavioural disorders to be the most conspicuous manifestations of abnormality in brain-injured children. Most of these disorders should be regarded as manifestations of exaggerated responsiveness to stimuli. It appears that the inhibiting responses which are normally built into the nervous system may be interfered with. The young brain-injured child reacts in a manner which is beyond the reach of effective cortical control.

A general picture of such behavioural disorders was given by Strauss and Lehtinen who found that the brain-injured group as opposed to the normal were erratic, unco-ordinated, uncontrolled, uninhibited and socially unacceptable. Another characteristic behaviour manifestation is the 'catastrophic reaction' similar to one described by Goldstein in adults — when confronted with a task beyond his ability such a person may experience a strong sensation of rage, despair, anxiety or extreme depression, with all the accompanying bodily reactions. Birch refers to the same thing when he says that the conduct of the brain-damaged person may be 'dramatically unpredictable'.

Among the specific characteristics most frequently described are those of distractibility or abnormalities in attention span, perseveration and what is variously known as hyperactivity or the hyperkinetic syndrome.

Distractibility

Teachers and other observers have commented on the short attention span of brain-damaged children, here labelled as 'distractible'. It is assumed that such children lack cortical control which prevents them from being able to attend to a given stimulus or group of stimuli for a sufficient period to make an appropriate intellectual response. Instead, these children appear to be reacting constantly to inessential stimuli, whether these are visual, auditory or tactile. This results in an abnormally interrupted cognitive development, since the child has difficulty in focusing and maintaining attention.

'Perseveration'

On the other hand, these children may also be characterised by a disturbance known as 'perseveration', that is the attention to a simple stimulus for long periods of time. Examples of such behaviour would include the child in the classroom who in writing seems unable to initiate a new sequence of acts and repeats the letter he has just completed.

While a child may appear to have a short attention span, perseveration may have some of the opposite characteristics, and it is probably better to describe his attention as 'capricious'.

Hyperactivity

Not all children who are called 'brain-damaged' are hyperactive, but hyperactive children constitute a significant percentage of the total group of brain-injured and pose one of the major problems to the teacher. One aspect of hyperactivity has already been discussed, that is, the sensory hyperactivity described above. The majority of those who use the term, however, are thinking largely of its second aspect, that is, of motor hyperactivity; possibly more correctly called 'motor disinhibition', which is the inability of the child to react to a stimulus which produces a motor response.

The hyperkinetic syndrome is characterised by severe and disorganised overactivity. While such a child may not be more active than the ordinary child, his activity is irrelevant and without clear direction. Also such children may be impulsive and meddlesome; they must move, touch and handle objects and are often destructive. This uninhibited behaviour may affect several aspects of their social functioning so that while they may appear cheerful and over-friendly they generally do not get on well with other children, are often aggressive and may display outbursts of rage. This behaviour is most striking in the first year or so of school when it is seen in 1 or 2 per cent of children who are often found to have fits (Rutter, 1966). In middle or later childhood this over-active pattern of behaviour is often gradually replaced by an inert under-activity.

Rethinking the Concept of the Brain-Damaged Child

The above account covers some of the most striking features generally accepted as characteristic of the 'brain-damaged child', but does not solve the problem of confused terminology. We suggest rethinking the term 'brain-damaged child' along the lines put forward by Rutter (ibid.). Rutter suggests that the term can be used in a general way to cover a number of different syndromes or patterns of difficulty which are the result of some impaired functioning of the brain. This use of the term would include two broad groups:

1. those 'involving definite abnormalities of function' (such as cerebral palsy and epilepsy); and
2. those in which there are 'limits or delays in the development of normal functions'.

In the latter cases it may be very difficult to determine whether the disorders are due to brain damage or just to maturational delay. More boys are affected than girls in both cases. Rutter suggested four main syndromes of developmental disorders.

(a) Retardation of Speech Development (Developmental Dysphasia)
This may result in lack of speech or understanding of sounds or a delay

in the acquisition of speech. Difficulties in reading may occur together with a lack of concentration and a delay in the development of logical and abstract thought. This is much commoner in boys than girls.

(b) Severe Clumsiness (Developmental Dyspraxia)

Here the child is backward, ungainly and maladroit in fine and gross motor skills (doing up buttons and laces, catching and kicking a ball or gymnastic games), may have difficulties of perception of shapes and delays in speech and reading. However, these are not usually permanent disorders.

(c) Reading Retardation (Developmental Dyslexia)

Here many of the above-mentioned difficulties occur, more often in boys than girls. Difficulties of distinguishing right and left, motor impersistence — the inability to sustain a voluntarily initiated motor act such as keeping the eye closed, and problems of concentration.

(d) The Hyperkinetic Syndrome

This has been outlined above.

Defined in this way, therefore, brain damage can be seen as a very varied and common problem affecting up to 5 per cent of all children. It is more acceptable as a definition than earlier restricted and misleading ones because, although broadly based, it is clear.

The specific learning disorders of such children, and those with cerebral palsy in particular will now be discussed and suggestions made for their remedy.

Incidence of Visuo-Perceptual and Visuo-Motor Disorders in the Different Types of Cerebral Palsy

The three main types of CP, divided according to the motor disorder involved are spasticity, which forms 80 per cent of the CP population, athetosis, which forms 15 per cent, and ataxia. A review of the findings by Abercrombie (1964) shows that where there is a spastic disorder of movement there is also a greater than average difficulty with visuo-motor tasks, in some cases slight and imperceptible, in others severe and permanent. Visuo-motor disorders are less frequent and less severe in children with athetosis.

Two distinct types of disorder may be involved in cerebral palsy; visuo-perceptual disorders (the impaired ability to perceive spatial relationships) and visuo-motor or constructional disorders.

Visuo-Perceptual Disorders

Studies of the perceptual ability of cerebral palsied subjects – Strauss and Lehtinen (1947), Dunsdon (1952), Cruickshank, Bice and Wallen (1957) – indicate that children with cerebral palsy and spastic children in particular have a poorer perceptual ability than the normal child. Most studies relate this, not to cerebral palsy, but to levels of intelligence in the child. The main deficits found are the inability to distinguish figure from ground and the inability to organise individual stimuli into a whole. The tasks which these children find difficult in practical learning terms, therefore, are the matching of objects and processes of abstraction. In reading there is difficulty in the recognition of familiar words (the tendency being to confuse words with similar configurations of letters) and there is a tendency to omit letters. Among the most widely known tests which claim to examine these difficulties is the Frostig Developmental Test of Visual Perception (DTVP) which deals with problems of position in space, spatial relationship, perceptual constancy and the relation of figure to background. Factor analytic studies, however, have refuted the claim that five separate areas of visual perception and visuo-motor skills are identified by the DTVP.

Visuo-Motor Disorders

Visuo-motor skills may be defined as those skills requiring movement under visual control. The difficulties that the CP child may show in copying a pattern or a shape include the failure to get the size and position of the angles correctly and a change of direction at the angles. The tendency to reproduce a mirror image of a model is also common. An inability to synthesise the information as a whole is evident. Tests for these disorders include the sub-tests of the DTVP, the Goldstein-Scheerer tests and the object assembly tests of the WISC. There is no doubt as to whether a visuo-motor disorder represents a developmental lag or a permanent disturbance, and what effect other sensory and motor handicaps have upon it is not clear.

Relationship of Disorders to Other Handicaps

Visual defects, especially occulo-motor weaknesses, occur in over 50 per cent of the cerebral palsy population and these include errors of refraction, visual field defects, various developmental anomalies and disorders of the movement of the eyeball (disorders of vergence and version) and difficulties of fixation – Smith (1963), Abercrombie (1963), Haskell (1965, 1972). Hebb has pointed out that 'eye movements contribute essentially to perceptual integration' and it has been

Figure 6. The Practical Effect of a Visuo-perceptual Disorder
A.   A 13-Year Old Boy's Attempts at Drawing a Bicycle

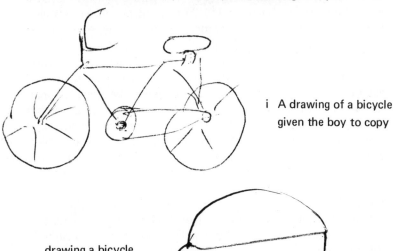

i   A drawing of a bicycle
    given the boy to copy

drawing a bicycle

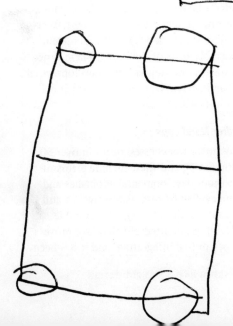

iii   His second attempt

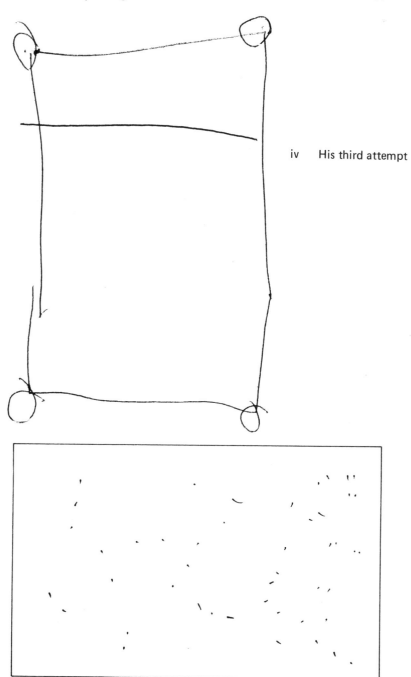

iv   His third attempt

The same boy's attempt to reproduce a straight dotted
line: . . . .

shown that CP children are less efficient than normal children in following horizontal moving targets, so that the relationship of eye movements to CP disorders needs to be further examined.

Motor handicaps may have two possible effects on perceptual learning in CP children. Although by themselves they do not produce perceptual impairment, they may cause a poverty of sensory experience, due to the restriction of contact with the physical world. They may also cause a distortion of sensory input due to weak, restricted or disordered bodily movements. Further research is necessary here.

Educational Problems and their Remediation

The practical effects of the disorders outlined above as regards learning are many. Caldwell (1956) listed the effects of lack of spatial ability in CP schoolchildren which hindered their normal development as the following: difficulties in realisation of position and direction with regard to self; dressing difficulties; difficulties with apparatus involving comparisons of colour, shape and size; difficulties in drawing, tracing, copying and writing; the reading difficulties outlined earlier and difficulties in number work of counting and grouping.

Remedial Programmes

Strauss and Lehtinen suggested that visual-motor perception in the brain-damaged child could be strengthened in the pre-writing phase by tasks which accentuated the differences of figure and background. They used colour to help the integration of perceptual patterns and beads to facilitate the abstract process of counting. They included the motor activity of the child wherever possible. Cruickshank has concentrated in particular on the behaviour disturbances of the brain-damaged child. He first assesses the level of ability of the child then provides a remedial programme which reflects his disorders. The programme is highly structured and allows conditioning to take place. The classrooms are designed to reduce distracting stimuli and have monotone rooms with typewriter, walls, furniture, wood-work and floor coverings all the same colour. Windows may have opaque glass to reduce stimuli from outside, and the room may be sound-proofed and have wall-to-wall carpeting. Tasks are approached in order of increasing difficulty for hyperactive children with a strictness of regime that reduces the possibilities of behaviour problems. Generally, the children are treated in an authoritarian manner and there is a strict frame of discipline.

Kephart (1960) concentrates on the large motor components of visuo-motor tasks and provides a series of exercises to develop gross

Figure 7

The effects of visual-motor disorders in the attempts of a 10-year old spastic girl of below average ability, to draw:
 i A woman
ii A house

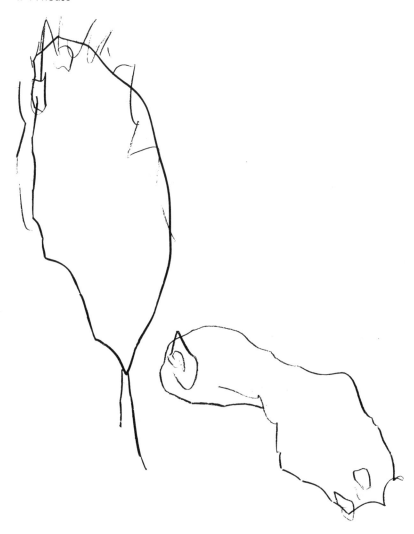

muscle movements, and skills of direction and orientation by means of aids or prompts which are gradually reduced. In Britain, Dr Morgenstern (1967), has produced a series of developmental toys for handicapped children.

In Britain and some European countries the programmes widely used are 'Training in Basic Cognitive Skills' and 'Training in Motor Skills' – Haskell and Paull (1973). These programmes consist of a series of booklets for children involving carefully graded exercises to help develop skills of perception, concept formation, abstract reasoning and writing. The essential way in which these programmes differ from others, particularly those from America, is that they offer the teacher a systematic and structured basis on which to build her pre-three Rs instruction. The teacher is encouraged to adapt it to individual children's needs. 'It is not a substitute for the teaching of reading programmes or approach to the three Rs within a classroom.'

The training programme for motor skills provides systematic and graded exercises designed to train children to develop eye-hand coordination and pre-writing skills. For example, the exercises begin with requiring a child to draw a straight line between two wide 'tramlines'; the child then progresses by drawing curves and angles, which eventually lead to the reproduction of individual letters of the alphabet.

5 MOTOR LEARNING

Physical motor development in children — and its relationship to ,
potential learning — is a large topic. Here we provide a description of the
key issues of motor skill development as a background to understanding
movement disorder in physically handicapped children. The relationship between cognitive learning and movement is also discussed, and
we will refer to cerebral palsy in children since these children exemplify
the problems of motor disordered children in a dramatic way. An
exhaustive review of the literature is impractical so attention will be
drawn only to those studies which are theoretical and of practical
interest to teachers and others involved in the management of motor
handicapped children.

At this point, it is necessary to define terms which will be used in
the chapter.

> *Motor:* by motor is meant physical action — initiated by the nerves
> from the central nervous system to the muscles and glands. 'Motor'
> refers particularly to the activities of the muscles and glands them-
> selves.
> *Behaviour:* 'Those activities of an organism that can be observed by
> another organism or an experimenter's instrument' (Hilgard and
> Atkinson, 1967).
> *Gross Motor Movements:* these are typified by games and outdoor
> sports and include such activities as running, jumping and skipping.
> The body is required to move through space. Strength is needed for
> these movements.
> *Fine Motor Movements:* these require co-ordination, speed and/or
> precision. Intricate adjustments in the body are also needed.
> Examples of fine motor movements are writing and drawing.

Both fine and gross motor skills can be studied in terms of spatial
precision, locomotion, timing and strength, but some research workers
find little relationship between the two types of skills.

Until recently there has been only the most limited interest shown
in the area of motor skill development, compared with the traditional
subjects of interest such as perception, memory and language. The
long-held maturational approach to child development has been partly

responsible for this. Recently, however, motor-handicapped and neuro-logically impaired children have attracted greater attention from psychologists. This is a small but significant step forward and, it is hoped, from these theoretical and experimental studies sounder in-structional techniques will follow.

One of the problems facing psychologists is that of adopting an appropriate strategy towards an understanding and study of motor skill development and its relevance to the acquisition of higher cognitive skill. One reason for this difficulty has been the lack of theoretical models to generate hypotheses about motor skill development. More important, psychologists have lacked the reliable and valid instruments to measure manifestations of gross and fine motor behaviour. Nor were they confident in stating what behaviour should be examined.

Two main approaches have been developed; descriptive and operational.

Descriptive

The emphasis of descriptive methods is on classification of behaviour into categories. The behaviours under observation are examined and recorded in terms of their significant features. For example, in studying the spatial co-ordination of limbs the movement sequences, strength and duration of movements would be recorded.

Sometimes some degree of interpretation enters into this method but certain types of motor patterns, such as eye gaze and smile response, do not fit neat categories and cannot be easily distinguished. Schaffer attempted to quantify 'fear of strangers' behaviour by using distance from the baby in the crib as an index of perceived fear of strangers. This technique, in the hands of unskilled observers or a series of different observers, could yield highly discrepant results. Other measures based on frequency and duration of intensity of behaviour are employed in describing particular forms of motor behaviour.

The descriptive or normative approach can be limiting because it simply provides a chart of the developmental milestones, e.g. *when* sitting posture emerges, *when* palmar grasp gives place to fine finger movements. Important as this is, it must give way to question of *why*? The analysis of the operations carried out by a learner is another way of considering the properties of motor behaviour.

Operational

The operational method is that of identifying and analysing the under-lying mechanism involved in executing a skilled act. The human subject is regarded as one receiving internal and external information, storing, coding and analysing the information and issuing instructions to parts of the body to carry out appropriate actions.

The establishment of a smooth sequence of actions depends upon a brisk interchange of information between a sensory input and motor output by a system known as 'feedback'. The reduction of errors in motor skill learning is effected through an accurate knowledge of results and the individual's monitoring of his performance. It is argued by some psychologists that some children with cerebral palsy fail to appreciate and master even the simplest movement skills because of an inadequate feedback system.

Characteristics of a Skilled Act

The way in which motor skills are acquired in young children is still not completely understood. One approach to understanding the nature and development of motor skill behaviour in young children is by analysing its sub-skills and hierarchical organisation, and here we shall consider the features and organisation of motor-skill performance.

Sub-routines: A sub-routine is a basic segment of the total action of functional unit (Connolly, 1968 and 1970). It is argued that, for a child to achieve even a simple movement pattern such as crawling or walking or transferring food from a bowl to its mouth, a discrete set of motor acts must be learned, executed with speed and precision and chained together in a correct sequence. Moreoever, it involves more than a simple association of single acts to achieve a functional unit.

Sequence: The execution of skilled movements such as writing, running and playing table tennis represents the orderly unfolding of a sequence of sub-routines. Inefficient movements, on the other hand, contain redundant or unnecessary actions, poor integration of movement units (sub-routines) and an unsatisfactory overall plan. Skilled responses consist of a number of units of movement or sub-routines which are subsequently linked, invoking the temporal patterning and co-ordination of these chained sub-routines.

A skilful footballer's actions, for instance, are characterised by his ability to formulate and execute complex manoeuvres (movement patterns he has practised repeatedly). He successfully integrates the component sub-skills through an elaborate system of feedback. The footballer is in a state of dynamic relationship between the incoming sense of information from his own body (posture, balance and so on) and the execution of a skilled movement (striking the football). He rapidly monitors subtle changes (state of football pitch, velocity and flight of ball, jostling by opponents) and matches his action to the changing circumstances. This is accomplished by a series of rapid decisions. Anticipation and timing are also involved.

Knowledge of Results: During the performance of a skilled task, internal mechanisms inform the subject about his performance and thereby serve to modify his actions. Movements in themselves prompt feedback and information about error.

External feedback is provided through 'knowledge of results'. A number of research workers have studied the effect of feedback on motor performance including non-visual fine motor operations such as line-drawing while blindfolded, and lever-pulling. Physical educators have used games and component units of games such as ball-throwing to investigate this problem.

The greater the availability of information to a subject, including knowledge of body position prior to and during the performance of a motor task, the higher the level of skill acquisition. For example, it is more effective to provide children engaged in line drawing with 'right-wrong' information than no information, but an indication of the extent or direction of error is even more effective. Learning, therefore is a function of the number of practice trials and knowledge of results.

Active and Passive Movements

Active movements refer to self-induced movements, passive movements to externally produced movements. Held and Hein (1963) in their studies with animals and humans demonstrated that certain types of contact with the environment are necessary for the development of sensori-motor co-ordination. Kittens, severely restricted in their movements, but not visual experience, failed to develop normal movement discrimination skills; such as guiding their forelimbs towards an object. Held and Hein devised an apparatus in which kittens, reared in darkness, were harnessed in pairs to a bar device rotating on a pivot. One arm carried a 'gondola', in which a kitten was restrained. The passive kitten received the same visual stimulation as the active one moving about freely. The free kitten transmitted its gross movements to the passive animal by the chain and bar arrangement. At the end of the 30-hour experimental period, the passive kittens, unlike their active partners, failed on such tasks as avoiding the steep side of a visual cliff and blinking at the approach of an object. They were grossly inaccurate

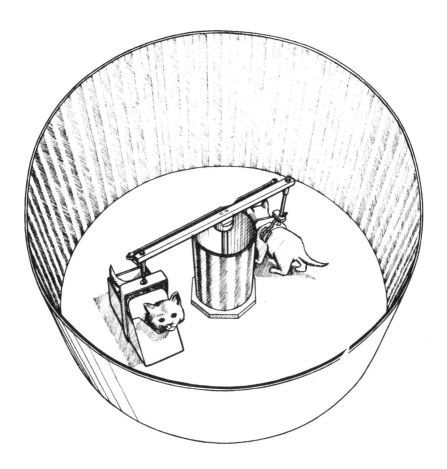

Figure 8. Active and Passive Movements in Held and Hein's Kitten Experiment

in their visual placing movements (such as the extension of forelimbs to avoid collision). The last response was elicited by holding the animal by its body and hindlimbs and allowing its forelegs to move freely down towards objects with interrupted surfaces. Refinements of this technique were used with kittens in experiments in which the animals were allowed to move about freely but without sight of limbs which were obscured by a large collar. The control kitten made 75 per cent accurate placing responses, whilst the experimental animals were only able to guide their paws accurately to the solid parts of the interrupted surface in fewer than 50 per cent of the trials.

Infant monkeys showed similar deficiencies in grasping visible objects if reared in circumstances which denied them sight of their limbs and bodies (Held and Bauer, 1967). Interest in the sensori-motor development of human infants severely restricted in motor experience, such as cerebral palsied children, is a highly relevant issue.

White and Held (1966), in a series of benign experiments using the technique of enhancement instead of deprivation, examined the effects of handling, i.e. cuddling and playing with babies between the age of 6 to 36 days, for an extra 20 minutes each day. Infants handled for such extra limited periods showed a significant increase in visual attentiveness.

As in the animal experiments, experimenters considered the importance of self-induced movements in accelerating perceptuo-motor development. They chose as their subjects young babies in hospital. White and Held devised a set of 'enriched crib environments'. They suspended toys, multi-coloured sheets and other apparatus to encourage babies to pay greater heed to their immediate environment (crib) and wider environment (ward activities). By lowering the sides of cribs and flattening the mattresses, the infants' head, arm and trunk mobility was increased when he was placed in a prone position for 15 minutes after each of three feeds. The babies were able to swipe at objects and take in more of the ward scene.

White and Held reported that this regime led to a significant advance of babies in sustained hand regard (increased viewing of their hands) and swiping (the tendency to strike at nearby visible objects). Children were able to do on the 60th day what, according to the Gesell scale, a normal child can do on the 84th. This experiment clearly indicates that the notion of a gradual unfolding of sensory motor skills in human infants is inadequate and pays insufficient regard to the differential consequences of early contacts in modifying rates of development.

Concept of Noise

An individual's ability to execute skilled movements is dependent upon feedback from his own movements — mediated by internal 'signals'. The process whereby this is effected is by rapid selection of the relevant information from the neuromuscular activity. It is held that children with cerebral palsy have extreme difficulty in filtering the relevant from irrelevant cues. When information is detrimental to the system it is termed 'noise'. If the noise is too disturbing or intense – be it internal or external – it can mask the 'signal', i.e. the essential message. Too much information or too little information can disrupt performance. Children with cerebral palsy may suffer from both problems (Connolly 1970, pp. 359-60).

On the one hand, these children appear to have difficulty in handling an abundance of information; they may find it difficult to focus attention selectively and to take in relevant information from irrelevant stimuli in the environment. On the other hand, children with cerebral palsy tend to lack kinesthetic feedback. As Connolly says:

> The problem then is one of augmenting feedback – such that the child can discriminate signal from noise. If motor responses can be brought under control by increasing feedback in another modality (visual) then it might be possible to shift control to kinesthetic/ proprioceptive systems by suitable training procedures (Harrison and Connolly, 1971).

Harrison and Connolly (ibid.) investigated the ability to learn to recognise and achieve a fine degree of neuromuscular control of the forearm flexor muscles on specific command of four normal and four spastic diplegic adults between the ages of 18 and 25 years. The subjects were provided with simultaneous visual feedback from an oscilloscope. The training procedure consisted of a graded set of activities in which the subjects were made to relax, then maintain light activity to command. Next, they were trained to recognise muscle activity ('spike activity') and achieve adequate control to avoid hand, finger and upper arm movement under augmented visual feedback. Finally, subjects were requested to produce spike activity at the command 'now'. No significant differences were noted between spastics and normal subjects, though the former group took longer to achieve discrete motor control. The results indicated that spastics were able to achieve fine motor control as normal subjects. It was hypothesised that a spastic 'can learn to control the hyperactivity inherent in his neuromuscular system given additional information concerning ongoing activity' (Harrison and Connolly, 1971).

The Components of Motor Learning

During the last three decades, 25-30 studies have been carried out in which the mental components of motor learning have been tested. Despite the attempts of workers like Ulrich (1967) to establish a relationship between mental processes (thinking) and fine muscular responses, it is very difficult to secure physiological measures of mental processes when they are used in learning physical skills.

Cognitive activities such as verbalisation and mental rehearsal of the various sequences of a movement pattern are called 'conceptualising techniques'. These have been studied in their effect upon performance of motor tasks in three main areas:

1. Imagery (the performance is imagined). Here the subject if requested to imagine going through the various sequences of a motor task and verbalise its movement pattern. Complex skills, however, involving accurate eye-hand co-ordination, such as ball games are not 'improved' by 'imagining' but require actual physical practice.
2. Directed mental practice — use of written or spoken instructions to guide the subject and describing the skill as one performs it. Cratty (1972) gives an example of directions given to subjects to throw a ball at a target in the gymnasium.
3. Mixed mental and physical practice — a comparison of mixed (physical — mental) with physical or mental practice alone. Cratty reviews the evidence of the effects of physical and mental practice on tasks involving hitting balls at targets. As a general rule subjects using both methods alternately become as proficient as those using physical practice alone. However, with beginners, physical practice proved far more effective than mental but there were no differences between the two methods in the skilled groups.

A number of generalisations can be made from these studies:

1. The majority of studies strongly suggest that the mental rehearsal of a movement pattern improves performance by two or three times the improvement in performance which is shown without mental rehearsal.
2. Mental rehearsal enhances most of those motor skills which are complex, involve fine movements and require the fusion of sub-routines. In other words, the bigger the cognitive component in the task, the more responsive it is to mental rehearsal.
3. There are, as one would expect, individual differences in subjects' reponses to mental training but these are not influenced significantly by IQ, verbal ability or sex variables.
4. Performance in most skills can be improved by means of directed

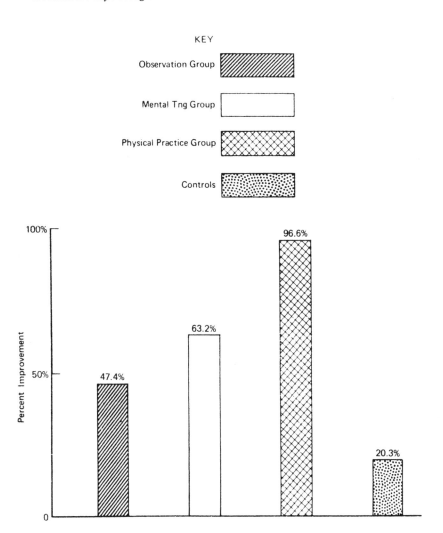

Figure 9
From data by Ulrich, "Some Experiments on the Function of Mental Training on the Acquisition of Motor Skills." *Ergonomics,* Vol. 4, No. 10 (1967), pp. 411-19.

or undirected mental practice.

5. Improvements in motor skill as a result of mental practice are a function of practice, task familiarity and the maturation of the learner.

6. Physical practice results in performance equal to or better than performance resulting from conceptual practice.

7. The learning of complex motor tasks is better facilitated when subjects employ 'verbal self-descriptions'.

A number of explanations have been put forward for the positive effects of mental rehearsal upon motor skill. The Skinnerian view is that 'finite muscular responses accompany conceptualisation of an action.' It has been suggested that imagining a movement pattern triggers off electrical action potentials invoking the very muscle groups which would be used were the actual movement carried out. This is confirmed in several studies including those involving eye movements (Jacobsen, 1932 and Oxendine, 1967). This is known as the 'carpenter effect'.

Muscular responses elicited by mental practice nevertheless lack precision, especially when the activity calls for 'well-regulated sequence movement'.

Lack of Interest – The Maturation Hypothesis

The neglect of interest among psychologists and teachers in the area of motor-skill development has been partly due to erroneous notions of motor development held by theorists of child development. Chief amongst these were the theorists such as Gesell, following the descriptive approach, who regarded development (including motor development) as a function of maturation. Environmental influences were considered merely to set limits to the acquisition of a behavioural repertoire. Gesell declared that 'development is a continuous process. Beginning with conception it proceeds stage by stage in orderly sequence, each stage representing a degree or level of maturity' (Gesell and Armatruda, 1947).

Gesell's view, that irrespective of environmental circumstances certain motor patterns will emerge in individuals, prevailed for several decades. Nowadays, as a result of experiments such as those by Held and Hein, White and Held (see above), this view is questioned.

In all Gesell's writing lay the assumption that nervous system maturation led to the orderly unfolding of motor ability in a kind of predetermined genetic sequence. Sometimes delays occurred in these changes – but the maturational progress remained unaffected by environmental interaction except by severe physical trauma (Gesell, 1929-54).

The conceptual model of the organisation of gross as well as fine motor skills resulted in a rather simplified account of the developmental process. It led to artificial and pessimistic beliefs that the developmental stages were invariant, followed highly structured patterns and were unmodifiable. As a result, the motor capacities of an infant were considered to be fixed and only marginally affected by his environment and not much influenced by such psychological states as motivation. In the case of children whose motor disabilities were neurological in origin, the outlook was even bleaker. Today this notion is discounted and attempts are made to educate children with neurological disabilities, in the belief that environment and motivation play an important part in the development of motor skills. Not only that, but the relationship between physical and cognitive development is recognised.

The Concept of Readiness

Interest in training motor skills in young children is not new. The Greeks and Romans were some of the earliest people to emphasise the importance of developing the intellect through physical experiences. The writings of Plato, Horace and Seneca contain references to stimulating the learner's tactile and kinesthetic senses when teaching reading.

During the last hundred years it has been the physicians who have been quick to recognise the therapeutic benefits of training the 'senses' of handicapped children, especially those who are mentally retarded. The physicians have appreciated that specific motor activities and specialised control movements are important and that the normal child learns by actively moving and exploring. Outstanding contributions in child development have been made by great educators of the past — Itard, Seguin and Montessori.

The early educators were unclear as to which motor and physical characteristics were important for learning: yet today we are no nearer identifying or predicting components of motor skills. The contributions of these great early educators have been neglected or lost. Their practical concern for 'remedying' disordered functions needs restating. A common thought of these educational pioneers was that movement is the basis of intellectual development. More sophisticated variants of this notion are held today and explored by psychologists and educators, such as Piaget. The emphasis of their writings is that many skills, including writing and drawing, demand a high degree of motor control. Most ordinary children develop this control if they are given sufficient practice, but children with movement disorders, especially if these are caused by brain dysfunction, may have less control of their body movements and find motor control exceedingly difficult. This inadequacy has led to the development of educational programmes based on the recapitulation of developmental sequences, where the basis of children's training has been the belief that individuals are susceptible to specific types of stimulation at optimal periods of their development. Much regard is paid to the unfolding of perceptuo-motor abilities.

The task facing the teacher, with regard to the child with motor handicaps, is to develop what Kay (1970) describes as 'continuous fluid movements, which are flexible and astonishingly rapid'.

The child's everyday actions need to be characterised by speed of operation and accuracy of execution of a set of motor responses. Physically handicapped children are often slower than normal children to develop these motor skills, or they carry out motor actions laboriously and less efficiently. It is important for the point of difficulty in the sequence of actions to be ascertained so that remedies can be planned to overcome this specific problem; for example, weak hand grip may be a cause of failure to manipulate a pen. With patient encouragement, physically handicapped children may be helped to achieve their optimal function.

SECTION 3 : PEDAGOGICAL ISSUES

This section is an attempt to relate the subject matter of the preceding chapters to the education of motor and neurologically impaired children. As it is impractical to include the whole curriculum in this book, four basic subjects have been chosen for discussion: reading, spelling, handwriting and arithmetic. Spelling, handwriting and arithmetic are subjects which have attracted comparatively little attention in research until recently, and still less thought has been given to these subjects with regard to physically handicapped children.

Each chapter gives a brief historical background where relevant, followed by an analysis of factors and sub-skills required for a child's success in that subject. ('Spelling' follows a slightly different pattern in this respect.) Attention is drawn to areas of possible difficulty encountered by a motor or neurologically impaired child and, where possible, lines of approach for their remedy are suggested. In the chapter on reading, no specific remedies are put forward as there is a large amount of literature on the subject already and because opinions on methods of teaching reading vary so widely.

6 READING

Up to the early part of the nineteenth century, the accepted method of teaching reading was alphabetic, where a child was taught the names of the letters which spelled a word. Then, in an attempt to overcome the problems of letter names not corresponding to their sounds in words, the phonic method was evolved, whereby the syllabified sounds of the letters were substituted for the letter names. The next development came early in the twentieth century, when phonics were supplanted by the look-and-say method, by which a child is required to respond to whole word units. Subsequently, fashion has swung back and forth between these two methods. In recent years i.t.a., the Initial Teaching Alphabet, has been devised. (See 'Spelling' and note). One may summarise research on teaching reading as having confirmed that the look-and-say method is advantageous for vocabulary acquisition but that the phonic approach is superior in all other respects. For a discussion of the success of i.t.a. see Warburton and Southgate (1969).

Ninety per cent of all children learn to read by whichever method they are taught, irrespective of the environment in which they are taught, that is, despite impoverished or unstimulating backgrounds, over-crowded classrooms and inadequately trained teachers in the teaching of reading. An understanding of the way in which reading is normally acquired is important for a study of the 10 per cent of children who have reading difficulties of various kinds. It is our opinion that learning to read is, like learning to speak, potentially present in all human beings, and that, theoretically, every child is capable of developing the skills he needs in order to be able to read. Any degree of impairment of the body or the brain will interfere with this capability and will reduce the number of necessary skills, relevant to reading, which he can acquire. As a result there will be slow, inadequate and apparent non-readers, depending on our definition of these terms. There will, however, be no child without some ability to read, and, therefore, no environment in which some form of reading cannot take place.

Three Viewpoints on Reading

The quantity of literature on the teaching of reading and on how children learn to read is enormous. It is appropriate, therefore, to discuss three viewpoints on the assumption that they most significantly enhance our knowledge of what reading is. These are: Piaget's biological/developmental approach, which defines the cognitive stages through which all children pass, Kinsbourne's contribution, which involves an analysis of human skills, in particular, those appropriate to the ability to read, and an attempt to explain the act of reading as described by Frank Smith (1971).

Piaget's assumption that there is a definite sequence in which physical and intellectual abilities develop in the child provides us with a set of expectations and a criterion of assessment for every child, handicapped or otherwise. The notion of a fixed order is reassuring, as is the notion of movement forwards. Terms like 'developmental delay' or 'early attainment' of 'milestones' encompass all kinds of children, the brain-injured and the gifted, each taking his position on the line of forward movement.

At the stage of development which Piaget calls sensori-motor, before the development of language in the infant, exploration of the environment through the physical senses takes place. The gradual awareness that events are repeated builds up expectations in the child, and familiar sounds begin to be associated with objects. The introduction of books, which can be handled and played with, encourages the perception of familiar household objects in two-dimensional form, and the sounding of words which correspond to the picture establishes certain ideas for the child. He begins to perceive that pictures and letters are both means of saying the same thing in different ways, that certain words or groups of letters represent particular objects and that the words for these objects may be distinguished from one another and recalled by their different lengths, shapes and configurations. At this stage, reading is a process of interpreting and gaining meaning from pictures.

The implications for motor- or brain-injured children, who may possess sensory deficits that impede their natural urge to explore and understand their surroundings, are that parents, or those to whose care the children may be entrusted, need to encourage as active a response as possible to situations in the child's life. Stimulation and informed encouragement, the provision of simple tasks and objectives and the familiarising of what may be a strange and incomprehensible environment (as the Peto method of conductive education attempts with children who have cerebral palsy) should begin early and be maintained. Difficulties with feeding and dressing and generally moving from place to place need not take up the whole time either of child or parent, if the priorities of intellectual activities are recognised.

At the pre-operational stage, according to Piaget, the child begins to make generalisations on the strength of his growing experience, probably seeing only one or two factors rather than all, and therefore making errors in his selection of what he believes to be relevant. With frequent exposure to print, however, certain patterns emerge in the printed word. The child begins to anticipate certain combinations of letters, sees smaller words within larger ones, sees words as having spaces on either side of them and takes particular note of beginning and ending letters. At this stage the word is mainly a visual image. The continued development of the child's own spoken language throughout this time provides him with opportunities of memorising and symbolising his experiences, particularly through the activities of creative play, and these acts of crude representationalism contribute to an understanding of the symbolism of the written word. The gradual awareness of the relationship of sound to visual shape follows and the child realises that words can be split into sound groups as well as letter groups.

By the next stage, that of 'concrete operations', the principles of 'reversibility' and 'conservation' operate. The child classifies objects and experiences in terms of differences and similarities, realising, for example, that a letter may alter its sound according to its position in a word, and that small and capital letters represent the same sound. He also learns to recall the sequence and position of letters, and realises that the same groups of letters in a different order mean a different word. Reading aloud helps to answer problems of pronunciation. Finally, at the 'formal stage', as Piaget calls it, sufficient skill for phrasing and expression is attained. The child adjusts his reading rate to the difficulty of his material, organising his reading of the text to comprehend its meaning.

Piaget's developmental model of reading acquisition assumes the presence of certain human skills, without which delays or halts may occur. An analysis of these follows, as an accompaniment to the picture of the normally developing reader, assuming that a detailed understanding of each of these skills enables the parent or teacher of the child with reading difficulty to prescribe remedial treatment.

The skills that many psychologists, and Kinsbourne in particular, have defined as determining the acquisition of reading are mainly perceptual. We shall also refer to other factors which are thought to affect reading progress. Kinsbourne describes 'beginning reading' as acquiring certain mental operations, each marking a stage in one of a set of parallel developmental sequences:

The child who is insufficiently advanced along any one of the relevant developmental sequences is not ready to read. If he has reached the requisite stage, then the better he is at the relevant operation, the faster will he acquire information (translating his competence into performance), and the sooner will he be ready for the next level of reading instruction. This level will call for new operations, possibly related to new developmental sequences. Whether progress continues depends on the degree of development of these new operations. But further progress along the previously useful developmental sequences is irrelevant. For reading, many processes must function at a given level of efficiency. Greater efficiency than this is redundant, because once an operation ceases to limit further development of the overall reading skill, it will remain idle while waiting for what has now become the performance limiting operation to be concluded (Kinsbourne – personal communication).

Reading: Sub-skills

This approach emphasises the attainment of a given level of competence at the tasks relevant to a particular stage of reading, without which a child may be unable to read. What these tasks or skills are thought to be are:

1. general motor skills;
2. visuo-perceptual skills;
3. auditory-perceptual skills;
4. speech and language;
5. concept formation;
6. intersensory integration.

1. *General Motor Skills*

Through his first movements a child begins to find out about himself and the world around him. These experiences form the foundation upon which his knowledge is based and play a major role in his intellectual development. His ability to orientate his body and achieve a correct posture whether lying, sitting or standing and eventually walking, will affect the degree to which he can handle objects with ease and therefore learn about their properties. Early development of flexible, balanced and co-ordinated movements provides a child with an accurate picture of his body and its relationship to different parts of himself and to other objects.

Delays in crawling, sitting and walking, together with unco-ordinated and clumsy movements and confusions between the right and left sides of the body have been shown to be related to reading retardation (Rutter, Tizard and Whitmore, 1970). Children with a specific motor and neurological disorder such as cerebral palsy, and those with minimal disorders of the brain, can be expected to show either severe or mild reading retardation associated with the motor disabilities or delays caused by the conditions mentioned.

2. *Visuo-Perceptual Skills*

A child's ability to steer and control the movement of his hands by the use of his eyes is usually referred to as 'eye-hand co-ordination'. Before a child has this he must first be able to distinguish his left side from his right side and also be able to control the two sides of his body separately or simultaneously. Initially, a child's movements are bilaterally symmetrical.

Accuracy of eye-hand co-ordination is necessary for the child's inspection of the printed page and the various directional movements involved in seeing letters and words in sequence. Confusion between right and left may mean that a child fails to scan a page of print from the correct starting point and sees no difference between a 'b' and a 'd'. Crossed laterality is sometimes found with a child who has reading difficulties, though precisely why this occurs has not been established.

The ability to discriminate between letters, to note the relevant differences and similarities in terms of orientation and spatial position, to be able to retain a series of shapes in his memory and the ability to distinguish figure from background also play a part in reading. Some brain-injured children are known to have difficulties in distinguishing figure from background, due to over-attentiveness to the background.

The presence of any defect in vision such as short or long sight, squint, tunnel vision or astigmatism may affect the process of reading for a child. Partially sighted children, however, can be taught to read well provided that they have sufficient skilled help from a teacher and sufficiently clear print from which to read. A teacher can do much to enable a child to use his sight effectively by concentration on essential features of a display. Blind children, by substituting touch for sight, can learn Braille. Tactile perception then replaces visuo-perception. Lack of sensitivity in the fingers, or lack of control in finger or hand muscles will impede progress in learning to read Braille just as deficiencies in sight or learning will impede progress in reading by the normal method.

Disabilities in constructional tasks, such as copying basic shapes

using matchsticks, defective perception of shapes and poor motor co-
ordination were found among the retarded readers in the survey of the
Isle of Wight (op.cit.).

3. Auditory-Perceptual Skills

The ear receives and transmits sounds to the central nervous system
where they are initially registered as noises with no meaning. The
child first responds to the middle, then the lower and finally upper
frequencies of tone, and the central nervous system then extracts
meaning from the pattern of sounds transmitted to it.

Auditory comprehension increases gradually in the developmental
phase which precedes the acquisition of speech. The young child uses
gestures and other visual clues to increase his understanding of sounds.
At the first stage, high-information words, such as nouns and verbs,
are selected by the child and stored in the brain. As sounds are occurring
in great frequency, the child must quickly learn to discriminate between
them and retain them in his memory system.

Poor performance in auditory discrimination at five years has been
found to correlate with subsequent failures in reading. Delays in the
acquisition of speech as a consequence of poor auditory perception will
also affect reading progress.

4. Speech and Language

Linguists believe that normal speech development is essential for the
acquisition of reading, and that this is made possible by good auditory
perception and memory. Learning to read must normally be preceded by
a background of meaningful, articulate and clear use of language, at
home and in school. Deaf children, however, taught from an early age
by special techniques from highly skilled and dedicated teachers can
achieve high standards of reading and written work.

The normal development of spoken language occurs from the time
of the first cry, the first production of sound. If there is brain injury,
muscles of the mouth may be affected. Consequently, swallowing and
general tongue movements preparatory to normal speech will be
impaired. At the stage of development when sounds are recognised
and discriminated, sounds are associated with objects and the use of
consonants is being gradually developed, so any hearing loss will result
in distorted hearing and reproduction of speech. Defects of articulation
will produce inaccurate and incorrect sequences of sounds, omissions,
substitutions and transposition of vowels. At the next stage, when the
sounds that others make have meaning and when the child accompanies

his own thoughts and expresses his needs with meaningful sounds, deafness will produce limited understanding of speech. Retarded motor development will also affect the use of speech in accompanying actions. Emotional conditions may cause speech defects — for example, hesitation or stammering. Skilled help at an early age is, therefore, essential for children affected in the ways described if later progress in reading is to be achieved.

5. Concept Formation

The development of language facilitates organisation of abstract thought. When a child names an object he associates it with sounds. Gradually he acquires a store of labels for everything in his environment. A child will have difficulties in forming concepts if he has difficulty:

> (a) in organising his perceptual information, e.g. distinguishing near from far or left-facing objects from right-facing objects;
> (b) in recognising relationships between objects in his environment, e.g. hammer/nails, cup/saucer;
> (c) in noticing common elements in sets of objects, e.g. that different types of knives (carving, pen, tea) are still knives and distinguishing sets or groups within larger numbers of objects, e.g. teaspoons within spoons.

The ability to transfer learning from one situation to another is also involved in concept formation. Reading is an abstract concept. Many children fail to understand that the spoken word is represented by the one written on the page. They have to discover that the written word has spatially organised groups of letters which systematically correspond to temporally ordered sounds. The acquisition of such a concept is related to normal cognitive growth. The brain-injured child has difficulty in developing concepts, not necessarily because he lacks experiences but because the experiences are not well integrated and cannot be manipulated freely. If he cannot make any sense from his environment in the ways described, he will be unable to cope with reading.

6. Intersensory Integration

Related to concept formation is the ability to integrate information arriving in the central nervous system from different sense modalities. In the process of reading, for example, information arriving via the visual field must be related to that arriving from the auditory field. As the child matures, his proficiency in integrating information increases.

This ability is related to the child's intellectual and maturational level, and most rapidly improves between the ages of five and seven, when most children are learning to read. A disturbance in motor ability, touch, sight or hearing will affect a child's ability to integrate sensory information which he receives from the stimuli in his environment.

Other Relevant Factors

For reading competence and progress other relevant factors are:

(a) intellectual
(b) biological
(c) emotional
(d) social
(e) educational

(a) Intellectual Factors: In a section describing reading readiness the Bullock Report states that 'very high intelligence on the one hand and very low intelligence on the other certainly have a significant bearing on readiness. But apart from these extremes early reading success is not closely associated with intelligence test measures.' It is also pointed out here that, later, a teacher's expectations of a pupil's ability may be significantly affected by the knowledge of that child's IQ. These expectations in turn will affect that child's performance in reading and in other subjects.

In the Isle of Wight survey referred to earlier, it was found that children with specific reading retardation were in fact of average intelligence, but their verbal skills tended to be inferior to their performance skills as measured by sub-tests of the WISC. Those groups of children which the survey defined as suffering from physical disorders (asthma, eczema, epilepsy, cerebral palsy, orthopaedic disorders, heart disease, deafness, diabetes and other miscellaneous disorders) contained a higher proportion of children whose reading was below the level expected on the basis of their age and intelligence than in the normal population. Apart from the asthmatic group, whose scores on tests of verbal intelligence were found to be significantly above the mean, the verbal IQ and to a lesser extent the performance IQ of the children with other types of physical disorder (except eczema) were slightly below the mean of the normal population. The authors of the survey felt that poor attendance at school may have had a slightly retarding effect on intellectual development and academic progress.

(b) Biological Factors: It has been frequently pointed out (Rutter and Yule, 1973) that more boys than girls have reading difficulties. The physical maturation of boys is much slower than that of girls, and therefore a similar biological process may be responsible for specific reading retardation in boys, through the slow development of certain parts of the brain. Goodacre (1971) also maintains that there are more very good and very poor readers among boys than girls, whereas amongst the girls there is a narrower range of difference. Although a biological explanation in terms of maturation may partly explain these differences, Goodacre suggests that as boys and girls have different attitudes to learning there are also different teacher/pupil relationships. Because girls usually begin to talk earlier than boys, they bring a more sophisticated level of speech development to the reading readiness stage (see Buffery and Gray, 1972, op.cit.).

(c) Emotional Factors: A correlation between specific reading retardation and certain patterns of behaviour was revealed by the Isle of Wight Survey. Children who were retarded in reading showed poor concentration and were over-active and fidgety. In addition, reading retardation was associated with anti-social disorders such as truancy, destructiveness, fighting, disobedience, lying, stealing and bullying. The explanation for this was hypothesised:

> The reading retardation handicaps the child in all his school work. Educational failure then leads to the child's reacting against the values associated with school. With status and satisfaction denied him through school work he rebels and seeks satisfaction in activities that run counter to everything for which the school stands. By this means he becomes involved in antisocial activities.

(d) Social Factors: The Isle of Wight survey established as affecting reading ability certain social features of the lives of the children it studied. These included the presence of a family history of reading difficulties or of speech delays in the parents or siblings of a child, family and household size which affected the degree and quality of verbal interaction between parents and child (i.e. the larger the family the less the interaction), overcrowded accommodation, the prolonged absence of the mother, either at work or for other reasons and the general attitude towards reading shown by the parents. Evidence from the Bullock Report confirms the importance of the attitude of the home towards reading in terms of regular reading aloud by parents and

such things as visits to the library.

(e) Educational Factors: A child who has pre-school education and early
encouragement to read at home will not necessarily be successful in
learning to read as a complex network of factors and skills is involved in
the process of reading and some of these may be lacking at any one
time in a child's progress. However, this early stimulation towards
reading should at least be reflected in a child's speech, conceptualisation
and general perceptual skills, all of which are necessary preliminaries to
reading.

Once a child starts going to school, regular attendance becomes
important. Some children whose physical disorders require frequent and
sometimes lengthy absences due to treatment or the condition itself
become discouraged in all their work, lose confidence and morale and
so fail to make progress. The provision of remedial classes does not
always have the success that well-intentioned planners hope for. The
extra attention to the reading problem may benefit one child but highlight for another his own deficiency and prove counter-productive.
Frequently, such classes are run by staff untrained in remedial teaching
and selection of pupils for the classes is made arbitrarily.

Other educational factors relevant to a child's progress in reading are:
teacher turnover, which is high in urban or educational priority areas,
co-operation between the home and the school in the reading programme,
and the presence of skilled additional help for the teacher of reading
such as a speech therapist or an educational psychologist who can
diagnose and advise on the treatment of specific difficulties. We suggest
that comprehensive records be maintained on the educational progress,
and the behaviour and health where relevant, of every child with reading
retardation; these should be made available to all those by whom he is
taught. Social circumstances should also be made known where appropriate. When prescribing treatment, the relevant history of the child
should be referred to as well as the diagnostic tests applied before
remediation.

If a child is learning at school to read in a language which is not
normally spoken in his home he will encounter enormous difficulties,
especially if his cultural background is not reflected in the reading
material. A large proportion of such children in a class will affect the
progress of the indigenous pupils. Special language classes must be
provided to cope with these problems.

Knowledge of a child's cognitive development and of the skills
involved in learning to read, as well as factors which may influence

reading progress, have been outlined. The third view-point for an understanding of the act of reading is the feature-analytic approach described
by Frank Smith (1971).

The Feature-Analytic Approach

This is a psycholinguistic analysis of reading, which assumes that a child's
innate cognitive capacity for language is an important part of his
ability to read. The ability to abstract rules from all the language made
available to him cannot, according to Smith, be taught. A child must
construe meaning for himself, not so much by being presented with
certain rules, but rather by being exposed to the regularities in which
the unknown rules appear to be exemplified. A child's perceptual and
cognitive skills then come into play and he discovers the appropriate
rule and how it works in a particular context. He must, however, be
allowed to test his hypotheses on the basis of the information given him,
and risk errors and receive appropriate feedback as to his progress. A
certain degree of inaccuracy is temporarily tolerated, although always
corrected, in the young infant learning to express himself orally, which
is not accorded to the beginning reader. According to Smith, children
are frequently prevented from formulating a potential rule in reading
by being expected to be accurate the first time and not positively reinforced for correct intepretation.

Smith considers that the basis of reading is what he calls 'distinctive
features', that is elements in the visual configuration of words and
letters. Although he does not say exactly what a 'distinctive feature' is,
we are meant to assume that it is related to the obvious aspects of
letters such as the ascenders of 'b', 'd' and 'h' and the curved strokes of
'c', 'o' and 'a', Smith's own examples. Any one distinctive feature
conveys some information about the letter or word to which it belongs,
though perhaps not enough information to permit its precise identification. The greater the number of distinctive features that are discriminated, the greater the number of alternatives that are eliminated. Smith
suggests that any five distinctive features are sufficient to distinguish all
the letters of the alphabet. Discrimination of barely a dozen or so
features may permit identification of a word among scores or thousands
of alternatives, provided the reader has acquired some knowledge about
which sets of features are critical for particular words.

The way in which a word is identified is through categorisation. A
category is a 'unique cognitive grouping to which particular visual configurations can be allocated together with a name'. Each category is
specified in the brain by descriptions which Smith calls 'feature lists'

that determine which configurations may be allocated to that category. A word is thus immediately identified by the discrimination of distinctive features which are then assigned to a particular word feature list which in turn signifies a category of word and leads to the word name. The way in which reading is slowed down, according to Smith, frequently by the wrong teaching method, is by the 'mediated word identification process', as he calls it. Distinctive features are discriminated, assigned to letter 'feature lists' identified in terms of letters, instead of word 'feature lists' directly, which then leads to a word name which in turn arrives at a word category. This method is slow because it is a matter of going from words to meaning, whereas in fact, reading is a matter of going from meaning to words, that is with a hypothesis of what might be meant which the words then confirm. This last point is confirmed by Smith's study of what the eye tells the brain and what the brain tells the eye. From this he discovers that:

(a) reading has to be fast since information is delivered by the eye in packages, four times a second, to a sensory store, the visual image, where it stays for not much more than half a second;

(b) that the reader must be selective, since only four or five items pass into the short-term memory, and these must be the ones that suit his information needs; and

(c) the reader must use prior knowledge in order to process the information in larger and larger units of meaning (i.e. not letter by letter).

Although this is only a brief outline of a large and exemplary piece of work it must suffice and the implications for the child and the teacher can be defined.

Smith's hypothetical feature-analytic model of how we learn to read suggests that a child will extract the information he requires provided that the appropriate informational environment is presented and that the child's visual system is sound. The appropriate environment is one in which opportunities are given to make comparisons and to discover what the significant differences are between letters and between words so that a child sees what a letter or word is not like as well as what it is like. Reading instruction can provide motivation and feedback, but the formation of rules is left to the child to deduce. The teacher of a remedial reading class therefore has to draw attention to those rules which a child has failed to perceive.

Kinsbourne (personal communication) has shown the deficiencies in a child's perception when he is overloaded with data and he makes some suggestions for their remedy. Kinsbourne's tests on beginning reading (personal communication) confirm that children most readily learn letters or letter groups if these are presented singly for successive comparison with displays which differ from them by single cues. In this way attention is focused without distraction on the crucial aspects of the array, one at a time. He suggests that failure in beginning reading is due to failure to attend to all points on a given dimension, and to all dimensions when more than one is represented, and to all items of a multiple display. Simplifying presentation to highlight a particular cue might indicate how children are overloaded with data, which they fail to interpret correctly.

Our picture of the beginning reader is of one who has the potential to learn, but who has many restrictions on the effectiveness of that learning. A teacher undertaking the task of easing the process of learning to read has to take account of a child's cognitive stage of development, consider his physical deficits where relevant, take social, emotional and intellectual aspects of the child into account, make a breakdown of the skills and weaknesses in terms of reading which that child reveals and provide the appropriate total environment in which successful reading can begin.

7 SPELLING

What is spelling? It is the use of conventional symbols as an aid to the reproduction of the spoken word. To spell correctly one must normally be able to hear speech, to have learnt the written form, retain that in one's mind and then recall and reproduce it accurately. Each of these processes involves complex actions and failure in say one of them will affect spelling performance. More will be said about specific difficulties later.

Most people, however, whether quick- or slow-learning, able-bodied or handicapped, find the spelling of English difficult. The main cause of the difficulty seems to be that English spelling is irregular, i.e. there is no correlation of either one-to-one sound/letter or sound/letter-combination. There are historical reasons for this. Old English in the tenth and pre-Conquest eleventh centuries was fairly regular and had two extra letters þ and ᵹ denoting the voiced and unvoiced 'th' sound. After the Conquest in 1066, Norman scribes, misunderstanding the existing convention, wrote English as best they could within their own convention, without þ and ᵹ , causing orthographic chaos. Added to the Norman French influence, down the ages there have been many influences on spelling: different dialects, including the effect of Scandinavian settlement in the North; anomalies caused by foreign printers and the effect of phonetic changes such as the Great Vowel Shift. This was a complex phonetic change which took place in southern England between the time of Chaucer and Shakespeare. Under certain conditions, some vowel sounds 'shifted', moving forward, affecting pronunciation, while the spelling in many words remained the same. An example of this is BOAT (shifted) and BOAR (unshifted). Foreign vocabulary introduced at the time of the Renaissance, later from trade and Empire, brought in fresh spelling conventions which exist alongside native forms. These were incorporated into English spelling which was not standardised until the second half of the eighteenth century. Latterly there has been the influence of American spelling. The result has been an interesting if apparently confusing orthography.

Nevertheless, as Albrow (1974) has pointed out, there is no necessity for writing systems to be related to phonology at all. The Chinese system is an example. In fact, the more recent the writing system, the more closely related to speech it is. For example, languages of the

Amazon jungle currently being translated are purely phonetic.

Firth has shown that language is a system embracing systems in phonology as well as in grammar. From this, Albrow has hypothesised that there are in present-day English fairly logical systems in spelling. By noting the environments in which symbols (i.e. certain letter patterns like ph, ch,) have various correspondence, together with the grammatical and lexical status of the items concerned, regularities can be found in our writing system which may not be at first recognised (Albrow, ibid.). The implication for teachers is that they should not tell children that a particular letter or sequence of letters 'spells' by nature a particular type of sound basically (e.g. 'a' represents the sounds in 'hat' or 'hate') and everything else is an exception, but rather that letters of the alphabet have many and varied jobs to do, each equally valid and important (Albrow, ibid.). The child is therefore prepared to meet different combinations of the same letters and to try out alternatives of sound when meeting a new word. He is also ready to take context into consideration.

The idea, however, that the apparent irregularity of English spelling is a main cause for difficulty in reading and therefore writing and the subsequent call for simplified spelling has a long history and dies hard. Does simplified spelling affect reading, itself a necessary preliminary of spelling? The National Foundation of Educational Research (NFER) wanted to see if children learning more regularly-spelt language made quicker progress in learning to read and write in their own language than those learning apparently irregularly spelt languages. The National Foundation also wanted to see if the way in which a language was spelt was taken into account when deciding upon methods of instruction, and whether spelling had influenced these methods. Accordingly, education authorities and educationists, in more than thirty countries, chiefly European, were approached for information on reading instruction and achievement.

The results were, on the whole, inconclusive. The researchers also examined other effects of spelling on reading in English. Six different junior-mixed and/or infant schools in London were visited, one girl's secondary modern school and three English-speaking schools in western Ireland. The schools were all in fairly working-class areas. The schools chose the passages to be read. The researchers found that, on the whole, less regularly spelt words caused more difficulty than regularly spelt words. In another experiment, ten nonsense words were dictated to groups of children who were asked to write them down in their own way as if they were real words. It was found that children in general did not relate certain groups of letters (graphemes) with certain sounds (phonemes) irrespective of context (Lee, 1960). Obviously much more evidence is needed before we simplify English orthography for educational reasons.

There has nevertheless been one attempt at regularising English spelling and that is the Initial Teaching Alphabet (i.t.a.). I.t.a. is an alphabet designed to help children to learn to read. It contains 44 instead of the usual 26 letters, to represent the 40 sounds in English. There is no q or x. An example of i.t.a. is:

"whær ʃhall wee ɕhauk?" askt peeter.

"Where shall we chalk?" asked Peter.

What is the effect of this on children's spelling as contrasted with the effect on children's reading? Two questions arise:

1. Does i.t.a. with its sound/letter relationship facilitate spelling when children write in it?
2. Does it confuse or help the child when he transfers to traditional orthography?

In a study by Warburton and Southgate (1969) the conclusion drawn from verbal evidence of teachers, advisers and schools Inspectors who had dealings with i.t.a. as regards spelling were as follows:

1. Infant teachers and all knowledgeable visitors to the schools were generally of the opinion that the use of i.t.a. for writing had enormously simplifed the task of spelling for children.
2. No infant teacher expressed the view that once they had made the transfer to traditional orthography, children who had been taught by i.t.a. were less able spellers than children who had used traditional orthography from the beginning.
3. The small amount of evidence on the spelling ability of junior children showed there was no clearly observed deterioration in the spelling of children who had learned to read and write with i.t.a. and later transferred to traditional orthography, although such a result had originally been widely feared (Warburton and Southgate, 1969).

How many of these would have learnt to read and spell early anyway is unknown.

The opinion of those whose work involves the teaching of spelling is important, but it must be supported by evidence before it can be seriously considered. Peters (1970) tested for spelling proficiency by a standard spelling test and a diagnostic test two groups each of 69 eight-year-old children, one taught by a rigorous look-and-say method, the other an equally rigorous phonic method, and compared the results. She then gave the same tests to 115 children taught by traditional orthography and 115 taught by i.t.a. and compared these results. This experiment also gave evidence for the debate on whether phonic or look-and-say methods help or hinder children's spelling. The subjects were matched as far as possible for IQ, social and economic status, sex and age. She concluded that the use of no method was superior in overall spelling achievement of children: however, differences of method or medium led to differences of perception which were reflected in the types of errors made.

Peters suggests that children who find spelling difficult and have been taught by look-and-say are restricted in their learning because they have visual but no rational reference: those taught by phonic methods are able to make a reasonable attempt at spelling a word which may well be a homophone (words pronounced alike but differing in meaning as — hair, hare), while children taught by i.t.a. have a basic structure from which English spellings can be developed (Peters, 1970).

In other words, i.t.a. provides the best basis for spelling development, but is not necessarily better or worse than other methods for general spelling achievement, since much might depend on other factors.

This research reveals important implications for remedial teaching. A teacher of remedial English would do well to find out the method by which a child has been taught and supplement it by other methods. If taught by look-and-say, try phonics: if by phonics, try look-and-say: if taught by i.t.a., try both. It must be remembered that most teachers teach children to read by eclectic method rather than by a single defined means.

The question arises whether a child, having once learnt to read, needs specific teaching of spelling to enable him to achieve spelling success or whether he will acquire it on maturation: in the words of a teacher, 'with sufficient enrichment in the form of the spoken and read word (provided that this is sufficiently active, emotional and meaningful)'. In short, is spelling caught or taught?

As a result of her research in Cambridge schools, Peters selects the following as being possible teaching approaches to aid spelling:

Apart from talk, being read to, and reading, all of which engender

interest in word forms, the essential elements to be taught are:
1. awareness of common letter sequences and the probabilities of these occurring;
2. the increase in the span of apprehension of letter sequences which necessarily involves —

(a) the use of imagery;
(b) certainty of formation of letters in writing;
(c) swift handwriting.

Peters tested children in the beginning of their second year in junior schools in Cambridge for spelling by means of a standardised spelling test and a dictation test. She followed their progress and retested two years later. Peters came to the following concusions:

1. Children with high verbal IQ and social and economic status scored initially better than less favoured children but over the two years the less favoured, by regular, systematic teaching and testing had more or less caught up.
2. The teacher's approach was of paramount importance: total time spent on spelling, regular marking of spelling errors, testing and learning tests, and drawing attention to combination frequency resulted in proportionate spelling progress. So did the practice of handwriting with a view to increasing speed.
3. Lists based on children's writing needs were more effective than published word lists.
4. Children whose teachers did not believe in specific spelling teaching progressed least or even retrogressed. (For further discussion see Peters, 1970).
(For further discussion see Peters (1970)).

Peters was testing children simply for spelling. She did not examine creative writing. Some of the most interesting written work done by children in the eight- and nine-year stages will have very poor spelling, for it is often the quick reader who has raced ahead in the infant stages and has much to tell who is not going to accept a brake being put on his need to express. It is our feeling that although a child should be encouraged to be adventurous with words and not be afraid of being wrong, it is unkind to a child to let him continue to think that incorrect spellings are correct. From children's writing, word lists can be evolved and used successfully, as Peters indicates. Moseley (1974) from his research puts forward the view that ability to master the full range of spelling conventions is largely independent of vocabulary development.

An example of lively writing by a boy describing a visit to a fair ground: '. . . then I went on the octopuse which is licke a sorspen lid that has just finisht topaling.' (Then I went on the octopus which is like a saucepan lid that has just finished toppling.)

A study by Personke and Yee (1969) comparing spelling achievements of matched Scottish and American children showed that the Scottish children performed significantly better, especially in the lower range of ability. The reason was thought to be a more formal and direct approach to spelling. Personke and Yee have also produced a model of the spelling process, which many teachers find helpful (Personke and Yee, ibid).

It seems therefore that children can be helped to achieve spelling success and that it would be profitable to try to help children who have special difficulties.

To spell one must be able to read. To do this one must have adequate visual perception to distinguish between the different letters of the alphabet. This is what brain-damaged children (for example, those with cerebral palsy) frequently cannot do. It has been mentioned that some brain-damaged children find it hard to distinguish between figure and background. Others cannot reproduce shapes or patterns (Vernon, 1961). All these limitations in perception will be reflected in difficulty in perceiving the lines and curves which constitute the printed word.

Certain types of brain damage in adults have been shown to affect ability in previously good spellers (Kinsbourne and Warrington,1964). Different types of brain damage have been shown to produce different types of error. Some patients suffering from what was apparently a disorder in language functions made different errors from those who had difficulty in processing information in spatio-temporal sequence (i.e. putting things in the right order). From this it follows that children with certain types of brain damage may have difficulties of processing information which will be reflected in their spelling.

Child A

Aged 14. At normal primary school up to 11 years.
Speech problem. Hemiplegic.
WISC   Verbal 87.   Performance 55.
Original work typed.

In 1973 we had kinkjan was it offer and the magers sein that the man who was in nueas and he was or the way out of course on the shep to the couns of the Austion nea Path. Back in the Amaers the was a sash paty to see if the man was near the pordey of Amaers and the costin

Corrected and Revised Version

In 1973 we had a message in the office. It was Kojak's office and the message said that the man was in New York and he was on the way out of the country on the ship to the country of Australia, near Perth. Back in America there was a search party to see if the man was near the border of America. . .

Comment

The boy is muddled in his story and his spelling. His speech difficulty is reflected in words like kinkjan − Kojak, offer − office, Austion − Australia. There are sequencing errors: magers − message, and in the order of the first sentence. In this case a programme based on the results of an ITPA test might be appropriate.

CHILD B

Aged 10. Athetoid. Speech Problem.
WISC   Verbal 108.   Performance 71.
Original work typed.

wesn a poner timethere was a squirr it was broun on it lived up a rev old tree the squirr leve nest he wesn aman cam wif a gun the squirr sed dont shoot me acoos i woot shoot you sed the man you are a derd little squirr

Corrected and Revised Version

Once upon a time there was a squirrel. It was brown and it liv ,d up a very old tree. The squirrel loved nuts. (He) Once a man came with a gun. The squirrel said, 'Don't shoot me!' 'Of course I won't shoot you,' said the man. 'You are a dear little squirrel.'

The Trip to the Aquarium

. . . . wen we wnt in it wos drck it hat little lis in it we cod hear the pims rarth like the typewrit. . . . . i hlop i go a gen one day it is cyit therer.

Corrected and Revised Version

When we went in, it was dark. It had lights in it. We could hear the pumps, rather like the typewriter. . . I hope I go again one day, it is quiet there.

Comment

If one is familiar with the Devon dialect, once can understand this. The boy's speech problem is reflected in the omission of the ends of some words. There are also errors in sequencing — next — nuts, rev — very. These pieces were typed so it is possible a few errors were made by hitting the wrong keys. Many words are spelt phonetically, in the way he would say them. 'acoos', wif, a poner.

CHILD C

Aged 10. Had home teacher previously. Totally dependent. No speech. This was done (the original) with a 'beak'.
Original work typed.

Jack and the Beensturk

Jack woas all a lon with his Mummy. they did not have einy muney. hes Daddy was ded. They had a cow. Jack sid hes Mummy we will have to sel uer caw. Jack tok the caw to market. on the way to market he bumped in to a man. the man sid where are you going wer that caw. Jach sid I am going to maret with it. if i gif you sum beans they are magic beans. He took thim home. his mummy took the bens and threw thime out of the window. In the moren they bekam a benstork. Jack went on it. Jack climde and klimde up to the top. when he got there he saw a road.

Comment

This boy is intelligent in spite of his disabilities. It is easy to understand what he means. Many words are spelt as he would understand they would be said — klimde, sum, ded, muney, einy, bekam. It is possible that with systematic spelling instruction, this boy's spelling would improve considerably. There are no sequencing errors and he has the sequence of the story correct.

One useful diagnostic test is the Illinois Test of Psycholinguistic

Abilities. Administered by trained psychologists, it can be used for children from ages 2 to 10 years. The revised ITPA, which is essentially the same as the experimental version, consists of twelve sub-tests covering the three main abilities needed for language usage, viz decoding (receptive process), association (organising process) and encoding (expressive process) (Kirk *et al.,* 1968). It is particularly useful for diagnosing language difficulties in brain-damaged children. Hart (1963) carried out an ITPA remedial language programme on 18 children. Pre-testing scores showed a mean retardation of three years in language development. After seven weeks the experimental group made an average gain of 13 months in language and 9 months in reading. The control group made 'only normal' progress. When the control group was given language training, identical gains in language age were achieved. In the auditory vocal association, auditory vocal sequential and visual motor sequential sub-tests significant gains were made. Hart argues that the ITPA's claim 'to provide a diagnostic instrument which leads to clues for remediation' is valid. From the diagnosis, remedial programmes can be planned (Kirk and McCarthy, 1961).

As mentioned earlier, there is evidence that in most people the left hemisphere of the brain is used for language. It follows, therefore, that damage in this part of the brain may affect language and subsequently spelling, especially if this damage has been caused by accident at an age when language functions have already been established. Although recovery of speech functions in infants with brain injury is greater than in adults, learning disorders and retardation in intellectual development often follow. If brain damage occurs at an earlier age compensation may be established and language functions served by the right cerebral hemisphere. The evidence that there are physiological sex differences in parts of the left hemisphere, certain key areas for language function and laterality for language being generally better developed in girls than in boys,has been discussed previously (Buffery and Gray, 1972). This may help to explain the relative superiority of girls over boys in certain aspects of the use of language, such as the verbal parts of intelligence tests. It also may explain why more boys than girls need remedial help in reading and spelling.

Present opinion tends to consider theories linking spelling disability to inadequate functioning in parts of the brain, without implying any actual structural damage, change or abnormality. Just as people can and do vary greatly in physical stature and consequently in physical ability, so they can vary in the sizes, shapes and organisations of the different parts of their brains, with the consequent differences in levels and patterns of cognitive, i.e. mental abilities (Nelson, 1974).

The best-known spelling disorder is commonly called dyslexia. Much has been written on this subject and many differing opinions have been expressed, varying from the assertion that dyslexia is a form of brain damage to the rebuff that it is 'a disease of the middle classes' and 'exists only in the minds of over anxious parents'.

Whether there is medical evidence for its existence or not, there do seem to be a number of children, otherwise intelligent, to whom the written word means nothing and whose attempts to reproduce it are highly bizarre. These children are not emotionally disturbed or suffering from any recognisable brain damage, the presence of either of which might help explain their difficulty. One can understand, for the spelling of 'saucer' how a child might write 'sauser' or 'sorcer', but surely not 'scaed' and 'sloy' and 'spiendce'? (Peters, 1970).

Vernon (1970) suggests that there are two types of dyslexia: the first is a disorder of language, possibly some form of dysphasia (impairment in speech); the second and more interesting type is, according to Vernon, characterised by some impairment of visual perception and memory. Children of the first type are those whose spelling retardation is accompanied by reading retardation and tend to have histories of delayed speech development, weaker verbal than non-verbal abilities, and make the sort of spelling errors which are consistent with language dysfunction (e.g. phonetic inaccuracies of the type shown to characterise the spelling errors of adult dysphasic patients). The second type of child has a spelling retardation but adequate reading ability. These children do not have a significantly lower verbal IQ than performance IQ on the WISC test and they make significantly fewer phonetically inaccurate errors in their spelling than do their contemporaries with reading retardation. Of the second type, the causes of difficulty are still largely a matter for conjecture.

One difficulty seems to be in perceiving the differences between letters, especially b and d. There is also difficulty in sequencing letters, for example 'asw', 'saw' and 'wsa' are interchangeable; possibly some fault in the child's complex memory system causes error.

Those children who have difficulty in reading as well as spelling often find it hard to relate letters to sound. Crosby and Liston (1968) advocate much time spent in letter discrimination, with a strong emphasis on phonic training for children with difficulties in perception and relating sound to letters. This method was used by one of the authors with a girl of 13 years who, although she otherwise seemed of average intelligence, was backward in reading and whose writing, i.e.

spelling, was nonsensical. Using Schonell's spelling list and by going right back to the beginning the girl began to make slow but steady progress in reading and spelling. This emphasis on phonics would not be advisable, though, with a child who had difficulty in sequencing, i.e. putting letters in correct sequence. In such a case a more visual approach is necessary.

Cotterell (1974), who worked for some years at the Word Blind Centre, advocates the following teaching principles for helping children with spelling difficulties. Many of them follow on from the findings and experience of other writers mentioned in this chapter.

1. Whether a child's weakness is in visual or auditory recall it is a good idea to take the learning off the weak 'rote' memory and place it on the ability to reason.

2. No word that follows an expected pattern needs to be committed to memory as it can be worked out.

3. Long words are not to be feared as they can be divided into short manageable bits (syllables).

4. It must be understood that every word and every syllable always contains at least one vowel (except when y is used as a vowel as in by, why, cry).

5. Words should be thought of as a collection of sounds and syllables rather than alphabetic letters (cf. Albrow). But alphabetical spelling is useful to help the weak visualiser master irregular words: in fact, as the child grows older, he often resorts to this technique naturally to circumvent his problem. If taught as suggested by Albrow the child will have been helped in his attempts.

6. To establish an association between speech and symbols it is all-important to train a child to vocalise (read it aloud) as he writes. This helps avoid syllable omission.

7. Crossing out a complete word needs to be tolerated because it is always best for a word to be written as a whole and not crossed out in the middle with letters inserted. The latter results in a distorted picture and 'feel' of the word.

8. Teaching of the phonic structure of language needs to be systematic with a certain degree of overlearning and reinforcement through writing. Words containing like digraphs, prefixes and suffixes need to be taught together so that they support each other and aid recall.

9. When he is learning a difficult word, a child should be trained to look at it, cover it, and then write it from memory, vocalising as he writes. If the word is used in a sentence learning becomes meaningful.

10. A child should be trained to enter a word in an alphabetically indexed pocket notebook and to underline the 'tricky' part of the word that caught him out. It is then available for future reference. He should be encouraged to devise his own mnemonics, as a verbal tag is frequently recalled more steadily than the spelling of a word.
11. Many bad spellers find knowledge of the spelling rules helpful. This reduces the learning load as rules govern hundreds of words. Every teacher should be familiar with the rules so that they can be introduced as the spelling arises.

As well as the above-mentioned difficulties, poor auditory perception hinders accurate spelling. Often a clue to this imperception is given in a child's speech. A child in one of the author's experiences had suffered a hearing loss as a result of Still's disease when she was learning to talk. The loss fluctuated for some years with the intermittent nature of the illness. At the age of ten she had only a slight resultant hearing loss but a marked speech defect. In her writing she persistently omitted the ends of words and confused certain sounds. A special speech therapy programme was advised and devised, to be carried out by the teacher. Slowly but surely both her speech and her spelling improved. Here a knowledge of the child's medical history was essential in prescribing remedial work.

To aid remedial work it is essential to know what kind of mistakes children make. Livingstone (1961) tested 125 children aged 9-10 years using Schonell Regular and Irregular Word Lists and Schonell Graded Dictation Tests and found the frequency of errors to be as follows:

Confusions	– dimet (dynamite), colering (colouring)
Omissions	– grond (ground), plese (please)
Insertions	– takeing (taking), warter (water)
Transpositions	– twinkel (twinkle), palying (playing)
single for double)	
double for single)	
Homophones	– reed (read), led (lead)
Perseveration	– perpersevseveration

Comparing children with below-average intelligence with those of above-average, she found the same rank order, i.e. order of frequency of mistake, but in different proportions. The below-average children showed a much wider spread of error, making remedial programmes harder to plan.

Glavin and De Girolamo (1971) compared types of spelling errors of 'emotionally disturbed' children with those of 'normals'. In two investigations both groups were matched on CA IQ and socio-economic status. In the first investigation the disturbed children made more errors than the normal controls. In the second study a different pattern of spelling errors between two sub-groups ('conduct problem' and 'withdrawn') of emotionally disturbed children emerged. Conduct problem children refused to attempt spelling more often than the 'withdrawn' children. The latter group reproduced significantly higher numbers of words with 'unrecognisable' spellings than children with conduct problems.

As well as Schonell's Word Lists and Dictation Tests which are a good guide to what can be expected of a child at a certain stage Daniels and Diack's (1964) Graded Spelling Test is also useful. Peters (1975) has published a set of diagnostic dictations which are an aid from which to plan remedial help.

In our experience children who are chronically sick are often weak in spelling and make mistakes several years later than one would normally expect. Looking at their mistakes in a different way from Livingston's, it seems that there would be a pattern which would suggest further research.

The children have had interrupted schooling and often seem to misapply spelling rules which they have only half understood, e.g.

Spelling	Correct Form
noes	nose (transposition)
thay	they (confusion)
mornning	morning (insertion)
sum	some (homophone)
don	done (omission)

These mistakes were made by children of eleven, twelve or thirteen years.

Sometimes these children write as they speak, having realised that there is some letter/sound correspondence, but in our opinion they lack the experience of seeing the word in its written form. For example:

Spelling	Correct Form
clectid	collected
Satday	Saturday
dressd	dressed
finly	finally

These mistakes were also made by children at the lower secondary stage.

Of course all children do this to some extent and these are not the only mistakes which children with interrupted schooling make, but the predominance of these mistakes may throw light on other children's spelling difficulty. Children with handicapping conditions which are not severe enough for placing in special schools, with the opportunities for individual programming, but whose conditions force them to miss regular schooling from time to time, may well be prone to this type of spelling error.

Dialect is another important factor for many children. If regional dialect, speech defect, brain damage and missed schooling are added together, it is not surprising that many children in schools for the physically handicapped have problems with spelling.

The lack of speed in handwriting which Peters found to be a significant feature of spelling success (if it is the cause of poor spelling rather than the effect) may be a source of spelling difficulty for physically handicapped children. In writing a word, a child who is slow seems to lose the image of it in his mind. A painful condition such as juvenile arthritis (Still's disease) will slow down a child's writing speed. This point also prompts us to look at methods of communication, such as typewriting for children (such as those affected by cerebral palsy who are unable to write manually or can only write very slowly). If means of expression on a typewriter or POSSUM* machine is too slow, spelling will probably be affected. Delayed feedback is also poor psychology in terms of learning theory. These points should be remembered and carefully considered in deciding whether a child should be given a typewriter or not. Attempts should be made to enable speed of communication and advances in the POSSUM equipment whereby phrases and whole words can be typed are very welcome.

Partially sighted children often find difficulty in spelling. This may be because of the lack of visual feedback, and hence the child's inability to retain an image of a word in his mind. A new technological development to help children retain the image of a word is the 'lightwriter'. This electronic display typewriter was designed by D.J. Bottison of the Medical Research Council, and H.L. Lowe and T.H. Gosling of Cambridge University Engineering Department. The lightwriter has a conventional keyboard but its operation is different and highly versatile:

As each key is pressed the character appears at the right-hand end of

*Patient Operated Selector Mechanisms

the luminous display, displacing previously keyed characters to the left. Messages move leftwards like a news-strip and disappear eventually as they reach the left-hand end. As the display shows 32 characters it can hold a complete phrase long enough to be easily read, in spite of distractions. A backspace key is provided for correcting errors and also a key for clearing the whole display.

Remediation such as Cotterell suggests is often helpful for partially sighted children.

8 HANDWRITING

Mans's desire to create a permanent record of his way of life was first reflected in his drawings on the walls of caves. This urge and the need to communicate with others has led, down the centuries, to sophisticated writing forms. These record not only messages but great literature, advanced conceptual thought and symbols of technology. In early writing systems, simple pictorial representations were made of objects and ideas. The step of greatest importance was the invention of phonetic writing in which sounds were given symbols, thus linking speech with writing. Phonetic writing became simplified into sets of two or three dozen symbols or alphabets.

It is estimated that the number of languages spoken today is approximately 2,800 — excluding minor dialects. There are three main types of character or symbol used in writing, viz. —

1. word-concept characters as in the Chinese language;
2. syllable-sound characters — as in 'Tulisan' in the Malay language;
3. letter-sound characters — as in the English language.

The eye movements required for reading these characters vary from culture to culture. They may be from left to right (as in our own), up and down (as in Chinese) or from right to left (as in some systems in the Middle East). Reading and writing are closely linked. The ability to read precedes meaningful writing. In modern technological society, anyone who cannot read and write is seriously handicapped.

In this age of typewriters it is sometimes suggested that children do not need to be taught handwriting at all. We disagree. An important reason for teaching handwriting is that the writing process is an integral part of the development of reading skills; the reproduction of the written form by perceptual-motor processes is a valuable part of this development. It is also important to be as independent of machines as possible and to be able to cope by one's own effort when the occasion so demands. Undoubtedly children now at school will probably not, as was once the case, need handwriting as a commercial asset. Nevertheless, there are many occasions when a typewriter is not available. Indeed, it is questionable whether one should have to buy such an expensive item when its non-commercial use is only occasionally required. A further argument for the teaching of handwriting is that as an art form it can be a source of great pride and satisfaction to all children, including those with physical handicaps. It must be recognised, nevertheless, that some physically handicapped children are so poorly co-ordinated that typing as a means of communication is the only sensible course for them.

Certain sub-skills are needed by a child to enable him to put his thoughts into the conventional writing system of his culture. The following are suggested for English writing:

1. the ability to see and perceive the shape, form and orientation of letters;
2. sufficient motor control to be able to pick up, hold and guide a writing tool across the page, with the necessary rhythm and fine variation of pressure to make handwriting legible;
3. sufficient hand-eye co-ordination to be able to direct a writing tool to form the letters;
4. adequate memory to learn and recall the motor pattern for each letter and, subsequently, word.

Inadequacy in any one of these sub-skills will produce difficulties in writing. It is essential to find out at which stage a child is failing before one can plan remedial help for that child who, though physically capable of producing legible handwriting, finds difficulty in so doing.

In any discussion of handwriting, the criteria of what constitutes good handwriting must be agreed. In the USA certain handwriting scales such as those of Ayres and of Freeman have been developed. In Britain we judge somewhat arbitrarily, taking into account legibility, evenness in the size and proportion of letters and evenness in direction of writing. Speed is another factor to be considered when teaching handwriting; for all except artistic purposes a child or adult needs to use writing to record information or communicate as quickly and efficiently as possible without sacrificing legibility.

Sub-skill 1 : Perception of Letters

Poor spatial perception may result in mirror writing, reversals (especially of b and d, p and q) and horizontal/vertical confusion (p and d). Difficulties in spacing letters and words, poor sense of direction and confusion in relative sizes of letters are also attributable to visuo-spatial difficulties. In the early stages of writing, normal children often present many of these problems but with practice and maturity these usually disappear. Handicapped children may continue to show these faults at a much later age than do normal children.

Interesting work has been done on incorrect orientation of letters. Schonell (1948) found that letter reversals usually disappear from children's handwriting at about eight years of age, slightly earlier than in reading. Boys were making reversals at a later age than girls. Chapman *et al.* (1970), in a study of 328 children between the ages of 7½ and 8½, found a similar difference between boys and girls. The children were required to write ten 'reversible' lower-case letters and seven 'reversible' numbers to dictation. Some children were still making orientation errors. Wedell (1973) observes:

> An analysis of the types of error showed that most were reversals. The most frequently rotated letters and digits were those which represented another letter or digit in the alternative position (d or 9). This indicates that a child is more certain of a letter or digit when it is meaningful in only one orientation.

Following from this study, Chapman and Wedell (1972) investigated some of the factors which had been put forward as contributing to uncertainty of letter formation. A battery of tests was selected covering areas postulated as being associated with reversal errors, viz. left/right discrimination, visual perception, lateral hand or eye preference, and knowledge of left and right sides of the body. From the original 328 children, two groups were chosen, matched for age, sex, school class and scores on a verbal ability test; one group (R group) made rotation or other errors in at least three out of five letter and digit writing tasks and the other group (NR group) made none of these errors on any of the tasks. Mean scores were significantly different on measures of only two of the tests. One was the Frostig Position on Space sub-test, in which a subject matches similar shapes in the same orientation amongst those in different orientations. The other was Kephart's 'Crossing the Midline' task which shows knowledge of left and right sides of the body. (In this the child is required to stand in front of a blackboard and draw a line joining two points, one to his right and one to his left. The points are arranged horizontally and then diagonally. The task was scored by a standard stencil fitted over the line drawn). One is led to ask why measures on only these two tests were significant, especially as the two groups of children were not significantly different in their knowledge of the distinction between left and right sides of their body nor in their lateral hand and eye preference and other aspects of visual perception. Body image and spatial perception seem to be important, but further research is needed. The R group's mean reading and spelling scores were significantly lower than those of the NR group. Wedell observes that the R group's spelling but not their poorer reading can be seen as contributory to their difficulty in writing. When the letter and digit-writing task in the original study was altered to copying rather than writing, from dictation fewer mistakes were made.

It seems that letter orientation errors are reduced when the letters occur in words rather than in isolation, as is shown in the Chapman *et al.* study, by the results from the Daniels and Diack reversible words sub-test. In their experiment, Marchbanks and Levin (1965) found that children pay most attention to initial letters in reading words. If this is a general truth, children would be more likely to remember the orientation of initial letters. This is tentatively supported by the Chapman *et al.* study, and the authors suggest that this may be one way in which experience in reading helps to reduce children's uncertainty about letter orientation. Wedell suggests that the R group's poorer orientation contributed to their poorer reading, which in turn led to their continuing uncertainty about the orientation of letters.

The link between reading and writing is emphasised by the studies described; the two must be taught together, especially for remedial purposes. There are perceptual programmes available for children who have basic perceptual difficulties — Frostig (1964), Haskell and Paull (1972). These, however, serve only as a preliminary to letter discrimination; the teacher herself must devise ways of enabling a child to differentiate between reversible letters and numbers. Illustrated alphabets in which the letters are incorporated into a picture of a word beginning with that letter, for example, are made to look like a worm, can help because the letter has a meaningful association for the child (see above). Series of words, beginning with the letters which a child confuses (for example b or d), chosen and illustrated by the child and set on opposite sides of the page, can be helpful. Hooton (1975) suggests methods of teaching basic letters, many of which can be used for handicapped children.

Together with these approaches, a careful observation of how a child in difficulty actually makes each letter is essential, followed if necessary with a demonstration at close quarters by the teacher of the correct writing movement. If a child is having difficulty in forming a letter correctly, an adaptation of a sand tray is sometimes helpful. A shallow box with a black bottom, covered with rice or uncooked porridge oats is placed in front of the child. The required form is drawn with the forefinger in the box, leaving the letter shape in black.

A quick shake of the tray makes the letter disappear. The contrasting colours of white and black make the letters easy to see, a useful factor for children with poor sight. Great fun can be had with young children with this simple aid.

Another aid for children with partial or poor sight is a pencil with a soft lead, making the writing blacker on the page. They may do even better with a black fibre-tipped pen. Lines may have to be drawn, possibly in green at the top and red at the bottom, indicating that one starts where it is green and ends where it is red. This is a gimmick that can be used for any child unsure of direction of writing movement. We believe that, in spite of current theory and practice lines are needed to guide children who are experiencing writing difficulty, if only so that they can get the proportion of sizes of letters correct. In a normal exercise book, heavy ruling of every other line helps a child in this respect, while letters with ascenders, such as h, l and capitals can take up two spacings. Copy books, now being printed once more, can be used (Paull and Haskell, 1977).

Books with wide line-spacing are also available and are useful for children with sight problems. An argument against using lines is that it cramps a child's natural style and size of writing. An enterprising teacher, though, can observe a child's natural size of writing and rule lines accordingly. If necessary, in order to guide the child, she can adjust the spacing of lines to increase or decrease the size of the child's writing.

For those children whose writing is uncertain and cramped and who need to gain confidence, writing patterns in the Marion Richardson tradition are useful. An adaptation of normal infant methods involving some gross motor exercises and large-scale writing and drawing may also help in this respect (Cambridge and Lansdown, 1974). These techniques have been used with success by the authors.

Sub-skill 2 : Motor Control

To help a child with poor motor control, close consultation and co-operation with his physiotherapist is essential. Exercises to develop the fine motor movements required for writing, for example, clenching and unclenching a fist, must be devised and a programme worked out and understood by both teacher and physiotherapist. Crafts such as weaving, modelling (the humble plasticine is still very useful for developing muscle strength and co-ordination), leather work, basketry and mosaic work all play their part. Also useful are balsa wood modelling, lino cutting, printing, constructional toys and clay modelling. Children with poor hand grip because of deforming or painful illnesses such as Still's disease find biros with round stems and with a ridge above the point preferable as writing tools to angular biros, which these children may find hard to grasp; they may even prefer the round-stemmed biros to pens, which have no ridge and require the fuss of refilling. The teacher could experiment with all kinds of unusual tools as writing implements for variety and for testing different aspects of hand/eye control and hand/elbow arm muscle control. Examples are: writing with large, thick or fine paint brushes, with fat chalks, with charcoal, writing with the length rather than the tip of chalk, writing with fingers dipped in paint.

As for rhythm and pressure, research, such as there is, supports the common-sense observation that, at speed, both pressure and rhythm vary, and increasing illegibility results (Harris and Rarick, 1959). A child must therefore know how to form letters correctly so that when he tries to write fast, because he is certain of the basic formation, there is less likelihood of distortion. A suggestion for an activity which would develop skills in rhythm and pressure, and is fun as well, is the use of an object such as a sponge or half potato, dipped in paint, tapped on to a large surface to a rhythm given by the teacher.

Sub-skill 3 : Hand-Eye Co-ordination

Basically, writing consists of a few lines: horizontal, vertical, diagonals to the left and right, and various portions of a circle. A child must be able to guide his writing tool in the necessary basic directions before he can write efficiently. There are programmes available to help children with poor hand-eye co-ordination, such as those of Haskell and Paull (1972), consisting of graded booklets through which a child may work systematically. Colouring and joining dot-to-dot pictures also help a child to develop hand-eye co-ordination, as does tracing.

Sub-skill 4 : Memory

For children who find it hard to remember letters and how to make them, continued, regular practice and drill, on the lines suggested above, provide the most obvious remedy. A child with neurological impairment will need much more rehearsal of writing movements than will a normal child, and the teacher should be prepared for much slower progress. There are many games and activities to develop recall of letters. Examples are: Kim's game, using letters; writing letters on the blackboard and then rubbing one off and asking the children to write it down in their books; including letter shapes in other work, such as lino cuts, painting, mobiles and collages; building letters in wood and plasticine; sewing letters in felt; using jig-saw puzzles with letters fitting into a cut-out background; using typewriters; using wooden or plastic letters, getting the child to feel round them, closing his eyes and guessing the letter; using stencils; making small size clay letters, firing and using them for necklaces and bracelets. It is also helpful to have many examples of letters in different colours and size.

Problems of left-handed children can be considered at this point. Left-handed children often scribble from right to left before they start writing properly. Wedell (1973) observes that if they continue to do this when they start writing, mirror writing results. He suggests that the teacher can remedy this fault if it is noticed early and the child is told where to begin writing. One must, however, be very careful to assess that the child is left-handed and still not ambidextrous and in the throes of establishing hand dominance. Too much interference at this early stage may result in stunting the child's creative and experimental satisfaction in the activity of scribbling — the teacher should not be too anxious to teach!

Left-handed writers have other difficulties. They have to learn to push rather than pull the pen. As they write, their hands obscure the words they are writing and this may make spelling more difficult to master. To avoid this problem, some left-handed writers adopt a hooked hand position, writing above the line. Nowadays, attempts to make a genuine left-hander write with his right hand are strongly discouraged. It is easier for a child to overcome the difficulties described than to write with his non-preferred hand. Hooton (1976), however, has observed that occasionally children are found writing with their left hands for some social reason (for example, everyone else in the family does) or possibly due to mixed laterality (i.e. dominance of either right or left hand is unclear) and are experiencing difficulty in executing letters, when really they have right-hand dominance. In these cases a change of hand is advised at least for an experimental period. Close observation of a child's natural handedness in other tasks and tests for mixed laterality might reveal this possible source of trouble. Normally, however, left-handed writers adapt fairly easily to the English writing system. Cole (1939, 1946) and more recently Clark (1957, 1974) have written about the problems of those who write with their left hand and make suggestions for their help based on an analysis of their difficulties. Three main points emerge from their writings concerning help for left-handed writers; the position of the paper, the grip on the writing tool, the nib of the pen (if one is used).

The paper should be placed so that the bottom right-hand corner is nearest the body. The pen should be held at least one or one-and-a-half inches up the stem so that the child can see what he is writing, without having to adopt an awkward wrist position. The nib of the pen should be broad, preferably with a turned up point or bulbous end. It is possible to have a nib cut reverse to oblique. Some ball-point pens are suitable for left-handers.

Various styles of handwriting and their suitability for the needs of handicapped children must now be considered. It must first be remembered that a child will always adapt a style of handwriting to his own personality. Indeed, a whole 'science' has been made of studying character in handwriting, although we do not consider this a serious scientific pointer to personality. Nearly all schools start children writing with manuscript or 'printing' style. The advantages of this style are that:

1. it most clearly resembles the printed word;
2. the straight line, the circle and spacing forms on which printing is based are more in accordance with motor and hand-eye-arm co-ordination of the young child than are the complex movements of cursive writing systems;
3. it is easily legible.

This style is usually abandoned at some point in the junior or middle school in favour of a joined or italic script because it is generally considered to be too slow for a child's growing need to write at length and speedily. The research evidence available does not support this general supposition. In the few published experiments (Hildreth, 1945, p.8) adults and also children in their teens, who have used only printed style, have written just as fast as those who used cursive script. It seems that children using printed scripts may be slower than those using joined scripts but by adolescence there is little difference in speed. More research on a wider scale is needed to verify this tentative conclusion, for we may be unnecessarily forcing children to learn two forms of script — a futile effort and a waste of time. This point must be considered in teaching handicapped children, who have to be taught so many things which are easily learned by most able-bodied children that the time spent in formal learning must be planned to the child's greatest advantage.

From an adult, at present, a cursive script is socially more acceptable than a printed one as it suggests greater maturity in the writer. Marion

Richardson method and style is one commonly used in schools because the style is clear and closely resembles printed forms. The disadvantages are that a few letters, such as b, f, p, z and x, have to be relearnt (although some teachers consider that a new form of b and p is an advantage as it reduces reversal error); letters with descenders, such as g, j, p, q, y, are not joined, and capital letters, which closely resemble printed forms, cannot be joined to the rest of the word. These two facts may compel a child to keep stopping and starting, which may hinder a child with poor perceptual-motor control or poor concentration. As it is an upright style, a child with a tendency to slope his writing backwards has no encouragement not to do this. On the other hand, if the Marion Richardson style is taught properly, according to the original teacher's manual, emphasis is placed on writing patterns, encouraging flowing penmanship and on the basic association between drawing and writing. Pleasuring results can be obtained from this style.

For those who have difficulty in writing, a new style was produced by Mullins, Turner, Zawadski and Saltman in 1972 — the Model Script. This is effectively the printed characters joined together and it avoids the disadvantages of the Marion Richardson style, namely the lack of join in some lower-case letters and the need to learn new forms of lower-case letters. As the new style emphasises forward slant, it is more difficult to lapse into backward slant. Every word begins with a downstroke.

Traditional cursive writing is still taught and can be very pleasing. As an art form it is effective. This must be taught at a later stage than other forms because it requires more skills. Some remedial teachers maintain that a change from printed to cursive writing helps weak spellers and there is less confusion of letters.

In recent years italic writing has been introduced in schools. This has the advantage of resembling the 'printing' style so that children can adapt to it very early and easily. Well done, it is a beautiful art form. Poorly done, it is a mess. Handicapped children should not be started on this style unless their hand control is such that successful mastery of the style is certain. Italic writing also has the minor disadvantage of needing a special nib.

There is no reason why an enterprising teacher could not adapt a style for the individual needs of a pupil, incorporating the advantages of one style but avoiding its disadvantages. For example she could teach a child to put loops on the y, g, q and z of Marion Richardson script if the child needed a clear style but found unjoined letters in a word distracting. An excellent short discussion of the general teaching of handwriting, including techniques of display, has been written by Dean (1968).

There are in schools a number of physically handicapped children who do not possess the motor co-ordination necessary to use a writing implement effectively with their hands. Some are without hands or arms. Some children, for example a few of those affected by thalidomide and some spastic children, are able to use their feet as alternatives to hands with which to write or draw. It is often found, however, that children with cerebral palsy, particularly those with athetosis, are unable to use any writing tool with hand or feet. In the best schools for physically handicapped children, careful assessment of the manual ability of a child is made at about the age of six or seven years when he has mastered some elements of reading, has had opportunity to use brush or pencil and needs to be able to express his ideas in some form of writing. A typewriter may be used if no other method of writing is possible. A number of sub-skills are required to use a typewriter efficiently. These are:

1. ability to see and perceive the shape and orientation of the letters on the keys of the typewriter and the printed character once it has been typed. If a child needs to copy or work from a book, he has to be able to see the original material, the keys and the typed output;
2. sufficient hand-eye co-ordination to select the appropriate key and direct the hand to the desired key;
3. sufficient motor control to press the desired key;
4. adequate memory to learn and reproduce the correct sequence of letters to spell the words required.

With reference to item (1) above, the disadvantage of most typewriters is that the upper-case or capital letters are written on the keys. This means that the child has to transpose from one form of character on the keys to another, i.e. the printed form, which is reproduced in the typewritten script. To help a child it may be necessary to cover the keys of a typewriter with the appropriate lower-case letters until the child has become used to the machine. He also needs to learn capital letters. Some teachers of physically handicapped children, however, have found that this transposition presents no problems.

Manual or electric typewriters can be used for communication. Normally a child needs to be able to direct voluntarily a thumb or finger of his own choice to use a machine efficiently. It has been found possible, when a child has been able to use his head only, to fix a protruding attachment or 'beak' to a headband, and the child has been able to type using his head. The teacher and the physiotherapist together should decide if a child needs a typewriter and whether a manual or electric machine could be controlled. A physiotherapist can also devise exercises to improve manual strength and co-ordination which will aid writing and typing skills. An example is weight-bearing on the hands.

There are a number of specially adapted typing machines. For some partially sighted children or some of those with visuo-motor difficulties, typewriters reproducing large print are a great help, overcoming the problems of being unable to read their completed work. One problem with a typewriter is that the results of one's efforts are far removed from the eyes, much further than with handwriting, and normal-sized print is difficult for some children to see. Magnifying glass devices mounted on the carriage can assist the ability to read immediately in cases where vision is very poor.

One school of thought, supporting the Peto method (described in Chapter 13), totally rejects the idea of typewriters, and by means of carefully graded exercises systematically trains children to be able to hold and guide a writing tool. To be successful, this training must start when a child is about three years old and be followed rigorously for several years. In Britain, where the programme has been tried experimentally in one or two schools only, it is difficult to judge its success. In any case, it is advisable to encourage a severely disabled child to use a writing tool as much as possible, even if it is only to write his name – a social necessity.

For some children, even an electric typewriter is useless and more sophisticated means must be employed. One major advance in electronic technology is the development of the POSSUM machinery. This can be used by severely disabled people to control their environment in various ways, for example, switching on the television and opening doors by electronic means using a controlled movement of any part of the body to do this. Part of the equipment is a large illuminated grid showing letters which can be used in schools for the physically-handicapped. This grid reflects either pressures from a joint or muscle or sucks and puffs from the mouth. A letter is chosen, a light is guided to the required point on the grid by a series of pressures or sucks and puffs, and when the light is allowed to stop at a letter, that letter is printed by an electric typewriter in the normal way. The main disadvantages are that the process is slow and the user cannot always easily see what he has written. Adaptations whereby whole phrases are written on typewriters by one action are a welcome development.

For physically handicapped children, use of other mechanical aids such as tape-recorders and cassette records in school can reduce the necessity for writing. It is particularly important that handicapped children can express themselves verbally both clearly and concisely; speaking into a tape recorder will aid this. Practice in using the telephone in as many situations as possible is also essential for physically handicapped children, as the telephone is a modern substitute for written correspondence. Replica telephones with connection wires can be bought in Britain from the Post Office.

Writing as an art form or craft can engender interest and give satisfaction to handicapped children who may dislike other forms of art. A well-known pen company in Britain annually awards prizes of pens and certificates to children who send in good specimens of handwriting and there is a special section for handicapped children. This is a source of pride and pleasure to children to whom awards and achievement are rare. Amazingly good results can be achieved by children who may have deformed hands. Similar competitions could be arranged within one school or a group of schools.

Very little research has been done on handwriting in relation to physically handicapped children or, indeed, to any handicapped children. Anderson (1975), amongst other things, compared handwriting performance of spina bifida children with that of normal children. She matched her subjects for age, IQ and socio-economic status. She found that, on the whole, spina bifida children did worse on a handwriting test than did other children used as controls and that performance by spina bifida children on the handwriting test was more closely related to IQ and other perceptual-motor tests than it was for normal children. Clearly, there is an unexplored field for research in teaching handwriting to both normal and handicapped children.

9 ARITHMETIC

The development of arithmetical skills has attracted far less attention than the development of reading skills in both normal and handicapped children. Up to a decade ago, over 12,000 research reports on various aspects of reading had appeared (Levin, 1966). During the same period, studies of disorders of calculation in both normal and handicapped children had been meagre by comparison (Haskell, 1973). The reason for this disparity is not clear since calculation, like reading, is essential for survival in both simple and complex technological societies. It is puzzling to understand why there has been so little research in this area when methods of examining and assessing the conditions leading to disorders in number operations are so readily available.

In normal children there are many and varied causes of backwardness in arithmetic. A number of research workers have considered the differential and developmental factors associated with development of skill in arithmetic (Dutton, 1964). These have focused on, for instance, arithmetic readiness, pupils' attitudes to the subject, level of conceptualising, learning strategies and cognitive styles. Teacher competency and structured apparatus have been studied and instructional material has been evaluated. Sex differences in arithmetical attainment have been examined as well.

However, before we can understand handicapped children's difficulties we need to know what the process of calculation entails in normal children. In arithmetic, a number of discrete operations must be carried out in their correct sequence. For instance, addition involves the organisation of digits in strictly conventional order. Symbols are employed to indicate the nature of operations to be carried out, for example, the sign + is an order to add. In all these operations unambiguous rules govern the spatial arrangements of the notation system. Sets of units, tens and hundreds are placed in vertical columns and, in our denary scale, increases in power always take place to the left of each column of digits.

Mistakes in vertical and horizontal operations or confusion of the visuo-spatial arrangements or left/right orientation disturb the most rudimentary calculation system. Examples of remedial exercises to develop accurate left/right, up/down judgements are given in the Training in Basic Cognitive Skills series by Haskell and Paull (1973).

124

Teachers could devise additional individual programmes which require the copying of columns of figures on squared paper. Children with intellectual, motor and neurological handicaps may encounter even more difficulties. However, it should not be assumed that a handicapped child will necessarily encounter difficulties in learning arithmetic or be permanently weak in calculating skills. We describe here the more important factors influencing arithmetical attainment.

It is not always recognised that home influences affect the arithmetical readiness of children when they attend primary school for the first time. Those fortunate enough to find school an extension and enrichment of home experiences tend to maintain the initial advantage they had over those less well prepared. A number of research studies (Douglas, 1964, Deutsch, 1966, Smilansky, 1967 and Chazan, 1973) have indicated also that depriving conditions at home (and indeed at school), in the form of lack of suitable play materials and appropriate language experience and poor motivation towards school learning can retard educational achievement in general, and specifically the attainment of number concepts in young children. It should be emphasised, though, that consistent parental support at home rather than social class or income level is a determining factor in children's arithmetical success and enjoyment. Negative attitudes towards school at home inevitably lead to poor motivation and lowered aspirations in children, for wealthy and poor alike.

Children with intellectual, physical and neurological handicaps make additional and unusual demands on parents; this factor may reduce their opportunities for learning. Early opportunities for successful training in arithmetic, such as counting stairs, sharing sweets and judging distances, weights and heights are, therefore, frequently missed (Haskell, ibid.). A combination of factors (restricted mobility, poor eye-hand co-ordination, restricted play experiences and fewer opportunities to learn appropriate arithmetic language) reduce the prospects of an orderly emergence of skills.

The introduction by teachers of such concepts as number, conservation of quantity, weight and so on, without first finding out what developmental level the child has reached is unwise and could hamper his educational development. There is evidence that carefully planned programmes based on a wide range of experience (Weikart and Lambie, 1970) aimed at stimulating and training cognitive and motor skills such as perceptual discrimination, spatial judgement and motor co-ordination can accelerate arithmetic abilities in young children (Brownell, 1941, Dutton, 1964). Uzgiris and Hunt (1971) have devised developmental scales based on Piagetian concepts, offering guidance to teachers in identifying these cognitive skills and the framework for training these abilities utilising sensori-motor activities. 'Rote learning' is inadequate preparation for a child to master the four rules of arithmetic; instead active exploration of the immediate environment, through play and other physical experience, is a necessary prelude to formal instruction in the class room.

Piaget's contribution to this discussion is universally acknowledged and enjoys a firm place in the literature (Piaget, 1952, 1953). He postulates that all children reach invariant developmental 'milestones', which are hierarchically organised, before mathematical concepts are mastered. In the early stages of 'sensori-motor' development the infant is dependent on perceptual information derived mainly by physical acitivites. Later, with the availability of verbal skills, he is able to progress through a 'pre-conceptual stage' to more abstract 'formal operations'.

Initially, at the pre-conceptual stage, only the simplest perceptual judgements are attempted. When he arranges and manipulates objects, rudimentary number relationships are established as a result of what he sees and touches. It is only after he has 'mastered the concrete operations stage' that he is ready to engage in 'formal operations' and a true knowledge and understanding of number relationships emerges. Piaget recognises that, although these stages are reached by all children, the age at which they reach them is influenced by maturation and experience.

Piaget proposed that the integration of information obtained from different aspects of sense experiences (sense modalities) serve to establish firm 'schemas' in young children. Schemas are regarded as conceptual frameworks containing the salient characteristics of an experience. These, therefore, provide basic organisational structures for the incorporation ('assimilation' and 'accommodation') of new information. Schemas are built up during successive environmental encounters, enabling children to interpret new experiences.

It is through the conscious exploitation of, and the experimentation with, the various play equipment commonly available in nursery classes, such as beads, cubes and rods, that children eventually discover concepts of 'more' and 'less', 'higher' and 'lower', 'longer' and 'shorter'. For a concept to become permanently fixed, the performance of the same task over and over again is essential, especially if it involves cross-modality skills. Bortner and Birch (1971), however, argue cogently that a distinction should be made between cognitive capacity and cognitive performance. Children might possess a concept but remain unable to make use of it because competing stimuli prevent abstraction occurring. For instance, in a simple matching task, when required to match a model object from among alternatives, unlike older children, young children are strongly influenced in their choice by the stimulus properties instead of the functional relationship of the alternative objects. In the Birch and Bortner study younger children were asked to match a red button (model) with a red lipstick case or a blue, round poker chip or a spool of thread. They relied heavily on the striking sensory information, selecting either the red lipstick case for colour or the round poker chip for shape. Older children chose by using the functional relationship represented by the spool of thread (Birch and Bortner, 1966, 1971). Birch and Bortner (1967) maintain that if the test conditions for matching tasks are altered, both for normal and brain-damaged children, and the range of choice is based on sensory properties, then the same children would find matching according to functional relationship easier.

Support for this notion comes from the conservation of number study by Mehler and Bever (1967). Two rows of pellets were set out with the shorter row containing more pellets than the longer one. As expected, children pointed to the longer row as containing more pellets. However, when Smarties (M & M) were substituted and the children allowed to 'eat the row of their choice, the children more frequently took the shorter row'. Bortner and Birch (1971) suggest that the capacity for correct judgement, though present, becomes affected by the nature of the object, the task demands, and motivation. In one case (clay pellets) 'more' meant the visual extent whereas in the other, 'more' (Smarties) meant more things to eat. The teacher should be aware of the child's level of development so that he can supply experience appropriate for him at that stage.

Another aspect of the nature of learning should be considered, namely that one experience, no matter how valuable, is in itself insufficient to establish a concept. As Harlow (1949) demonstrated, a single encounter offers a subject only the most limited opportunities of learning the rules or adopting effective strategies. Harlow discovered that, when required to solve simple discrimination problems, monkeys and children learn in two stages – a trial and error, and later an insight stage – provided that several learning occasions are offered to the subject. This observation is particularly important when considering the learning needs of handicapped children. It does not develop spontaneously but by laborious and systematic training. The success of this operation depends upon a brisk interchange between sensory input and motor output. According to Harlow, concepts, the raw materials for 'human thinking', require this rich interchange between the organism and its environment in order to become firmly established. The number of uncontrived and contrived experiences, both in the home and at school, and the skilful engineering of the 'arithmetical environment' of the young child by the teacher, will determine when and how concepts of number, quantity and space will be acquired. Activities such as setting the table at home and at school for the correct number of people and the arrangement of knives, forks, spoons, place mats, glasses, etc., which stress right/left, up/down discrimination provide natural (and regular) training opportunities for these children. Physically handicapped children are often restricted in their physical interaction with the environment and unless opportunities are specially created for them, they miss these important stages and experiences.

Consequences of Sensori-Motor Deprivation

At the simplest level, disorders of the sensory organs which affect vision, hearing, proprioception, kinaesthesis, tactile and other modalities give rise to disturbed psychological processes of perception, attention, conceptualisation and regulation of movement. In the more severe cases involving lesions above the brain stem, the effects on arithmetical abilities are hypothesised by Strauss and Lehtinen (1947) thus:

> the brain injured organism lacks the ability possessed by the normal child to discover spontaneously the significant relationships of the number system. Accepting the thesis that a perceptual scheme of visual spatial organisation is the basis of calculation, it is reasonable to anticipate that the organism whose ability to construct such a perceptual scheme has been disturbed will be hindered in any activities which require its use.

Cerebral palsied children, with disorders of movement and posture due to cerebral lesions, experience special difficulties in performing with proficiency and ease such functions as locomotion, feeding, dressing and sitting. Children who are severely physically handicapped also tend to be restricted in their range of purposeful motor activities and consequently their general arithmetical development is delayed. As mentioned earlier, Held and Hein (1963) demonstrated that in both animals and man, physical mobility, together with appropriate perceptual experience, is a necessary prerequisite for normal perceptual development.

It would be useful to refer to the work of White and Held (1966), which showed that infants raised in enriched environments (visually attractive cribs and surrounds, suspended toys, mobiles and pacifiers with interesting patterned backgrounds) exhibited marked perceptuo-motor precocity with respect to examining and manipulating their hands, prehension and visual attention.

Both in movements and variety of visual, auditory and tactile experiences, motor-handicapped children appear severely underprivileged. We would expect, therefore, that motor-handicapped children's intellectual and arithmetical development would be affected if the physical constraints of movement are so gross as to disrupt such basic cognitive functions as sorting, classifying and matching (Haskell, 1973). The consequences of reduced contact with the environment are serious and the resulting arrested development of sensori-motor skills increases the risk of educational failure. Parents and teachers could provide children with toys which offer a variety of sensations, sounds, colour, textures and temperatures. Toys designed by Anne Sokolow encourage exploration, compatible with the physically handicapped child's mental and physical development (Sokolow, personal communication).

Interruptions in School Attendance

Absence from school of both normal and handicapped children affects attainment in arithmetic more than in reading or most other school subjects. Schonell and Schonell (1957) maintain that because arithmetic involves understanding sequential steps and children progress by mastering each step in succession, the irregular attender who misses critical stages finds it hard to keep up with his peers as he has nothing on which to base his next work. Teachers should be aware of the feelings of anxiety which repeated absence from arithmetic lessons may create in certain children.

Haskell (1973) found that the use of Programmed Instruction (PI) for children with CP had certain obvious advantages when continuity of attendance during the term was interrupted by illness or accident. This method was also helpful for children in classes with excessively wide ranges of intellectual ability. Individual children benefited from PI because the pace of learning was directly maintained by the child and not by arbitrary standards imposed by the class situation.

Emotional and Temperamental Factors

Failure often leads to anxiety and negative attitudes to the subject, which in themselves may contribute towards arithmetical failure. There are even cases reported of repeated failure in arithmetic leading to

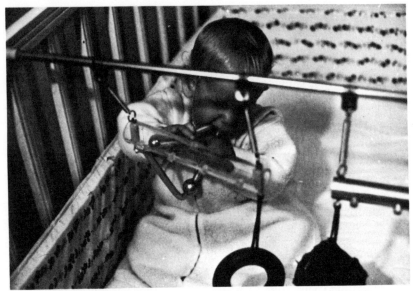

PLAYMOBILE

The playmobile strung across the cot enables the supine child to bump and to tug at the toys to create a variety of sounds and shapes. If the physically handicapped child is able to sit up and manipulate the playmobile by sucking, rattling and pulling the individual toys, gross and fine motor dexterity is developed.

THE FLAPPER

This simple and attractive toy is designed to help overcome difficulties of hand co-ordination, grasp and uncontrolled movements in physically handicapped children. The sound produced by the tongue flapping across the cogged roller has a special appeal for young physically handicapped children.

'HOUSE OF SOUNDS'

Photos: Anne Sokolow

This game serves a variety of functions for motor handicapped children. A simpler version has two rooms with transparent or opaque doors, to enable the child to follow the movement of the ball when dropped through the chimney. The house, with four rooms, consists of different materials (such as tin, plastic and wood) different colours and door catches, creating different sounds. Curiosity, eye-hand co-ordination, visual and auditory tracking and skills of memory, listening and matching a sound to a particular colour are developed by this game.

maladjusted behaviour (Gregory, 1965). Some studies by Lynn (1957) and Biggs (1959) indicate that children who are anxious or temperamentally unstable tend to display negative attitudes to arithmetic. It is not uncommon for some children to identify with the unfavourable attitudes of parents and teachers to the subject (Biggs, ibid.). In addition, where teachers are unsympathetic to a pupil's poor performance in arithmetic, the fear and anxiety of the child increases. There are indications that a child's temperament may contribute to success or failure. Some children, however, like arithmetic because of its orderly pattern and structure.

Active and Passive Movements

Handicapped children, especially those with motor disorders arising out of central nervous system dysfunctioning, require greater opportunities for physical experimentation in order to learn how to solve simple problems than do normal children. To appreciate abstract concepts, such as conservation, a child needs to practise activities such as re-arranging a collection of wooden bricks in space, inspecting and verifying its properties and studying the altered pattern produced by re-arranging a similar number of objects.

At a certain stage of a child's sensori-motor development, a normal child enjoys experimenting with toys himself instead of having an adult's helping hand directing his movements. This is regarded as a significant developmental milestone, according to Piaget, because the child is 'trying out' all the schemas available to him for discovery learning. A child with severe motor disabilities, on the other hand, has greatly reduced opportunities to learn by experimentation and the framework on which to build schemas is weak, because he cannot 'discover' for himself by playing and experimenting. For instance, a young child develops concepts of reversibility more easily when given ample play opportunities to re-arrange a collection of objects by reversing its pattern and then returning the objects to their original position than when denied this practice.

Brain-injured children encounter special problems in transferring from three dimensions of an object to the two-dimensional representation of it. To overcome these difficulties such children require skilled help and systematic training, and active participation by the child is essential. Learning by proxy or passive movements, i.e. when the physiotherapist manipulates the child's limbs as happens so frequently with severely handicapped children, is far less effective. Physically handicapped children need to carry out 'volume conservation' experiments with containers of varing sizes to discover for themselves by direct observation that volume retains its capacity and is 'conserved' in whichever shape of container it is poured into. It is through successive actions reinforced with appropriate language that true understanding grows, concepts and schemas develop and serve as a basis for mathematical reasoning.

Practice is clearly essential for consolidating a newly learned skill, especially calculation or learning tables. For arithmetical responses to be organised with precision and speed, children need considerable rehearsal in each of the four rules of arithmetic. The ultimate aim should be to free the child from conscious planning and long hours of tedious procedures such as recalling multiplication tables (Schonnel and Schonell, 1957).

Ocular-Motor Disorders and Calculating Difficulties

A high percentage of ocular-motor defects are present in brain-injured children (Smith, 1963). The frequent occurrence of refractive errors, strabismus (squint), visual field defects and various developmental anomalies hold in abeyance the normal attainment of arithmetical competency in young children. As Hebb (1949) has pointed out, much early learning is dependent upon the integrity of visual functioning. Cerebral palsied children with visual disorders seem highly vulnerable (Abercrombie, 1960, 1963, 1963a, 1964) to arithmetical failure. It is important to remember that whilst an ocular defect does not necessarily mean that the child will have difficulties in visual perception, nevertheless, alternating squints, severe nystagmus, tunnel vision, defective visual scanning of a set of numbers and disordered eye movements could affect simple calculating functions and other skills requiring movement under visual control.

Memory for Visual and Spatial Sequencing

Another function related to calculating skills is memory for visual and spatial sequencing. The ability to retain and recall the correct order of digits or composite numbers is demanded at the simplest level in a computational task. Brain-injured children have been known to experience selective impairment of this function (Kinsbourne and Warrington, 1963). The association between calculation and sequential difficulties suggests an underlying disorder of arranging a collection of objects in their correct spatio-temporal sequence (Lefford, 1970).

Distractability

These children are sometimes described as 'hyperactive, hyperkinetic or stimulus bound', being unable to ignore the variety of stimuli which they receive. When carrying out arithmetical operations, these children have the greatest difficulty in inhibiting their response to the competing stimuli of extraneous digits and symbols and selectively focusing on and attending to a limited field. On the other hand, these children may become unnaturally attached to a single stimulus for long periods of time or 'perseverate'. (For fuller discussion see Chapter 4 on brain damage).

Perseveration

According to Grewel (1969) perseveration is a

> general disorder which is found in all varieties of sensori-motor dis-
> organization: apraxias, agnosias, aphasias:, and may hamper calculat-
> ing ability. After an operation is carried out, the child may persist in
> continuing with the same operation, for example, after being asked
> to add 4 + 4, the child will with the next problem, 3 − 1, answer 4
> (repeating the operation of addition; or given 4 x 4 will answer 8).
> The child may get unnaturally fixated to a single number or
> numbers and ignore the requirement to perform the arithmetic
> operation; for 3 + 3 the child answers 33,or when asked 20 + 15, he
> answers 25. There may be persistence in rote counting. For example
> when directed to perform an operation such as 11 + 5 the child
> ignores the + 5 and answers 12.

Arithmetical Ability in Cerebral Palsied Children

Phillips and White (1964) noted that motor-disabled children with brain injury fared poorly on arithmetic compared with motor-handicapped control groups, without congenital brain injury. On the Revised Southend Arithmetic Test in Mechanical Arithmetic, the mean arithmetic achievement of the 23 cerebral palsied children was significantly poorer, after controlling for age and IQ differences, than that of 32 physically handicapped children without neurological involvements. Another study which revealed severe weaknesses in arithmetic as measured on the Burt Four Rules and Ballard One Minute Test in Oral Addition and Subtraction was the East Scotland Survey carried out by Henderson (1961). Of the 153 cerebral palsied children 93.5 per cent were backward, compared with normal children.

Dunsdon (1952) concluded that 'weak gestalt' (poor appreciation of form or configuration) as measured on the Bender Gestalt test was commoner in athetoids than spastics, and contributed to their lowered arithmetic attainment. Dunsdon studied a highly selected group of 35 cerebral palsied children, drawn from her own large sample of 916 pupils, and based her scoring on the mental age norms provided in the manual. In her sample, 60 per cent of the cerebral palsied children showed a closer relationship between their Bender and Arithmetic scores, compared with 46 per cent which showed similar relationships between verbal reasoning and visual memory factors (based on various items of the Stanford Binet, 1937).

Haskell (1973) carried out a study in which a programme of instruction which covered the four basic rules of arithmetic was used and applied over a period of 13 weeks to a group of 21 cerebral palsied children between the ages of 9 and 16. A matched group of similarly handicapped children was taught by conventional methods. Both groups showed gains in arithmetic and both methods had merit. However, restless and withdrawn children taught by conventional methods benefited less than their counterparts instructed by pro-grammed instruction. Progress in the four rules of arithmetic correlated with spatial and non-verbal items of tests.

Neurological Factors

From a psychological point of view, it is of absorbing interest to trace any link between cerebral insult and deficiency in number operations. However, attempts to establish causal relationships between localisation of lesion and specific deranged functions have proved inconclusive. Grewel's (1969) scholarly review of the acalculias (impaired ability to perform simple calculations) is recommended, and should convey some notion of the difference in views expressed over the last half-century. His survey (ibid.) of the clinical evidence for the localisation of lesion in the occipital, temporal, frontal and parietal lobes and disturbances in calculation, mainly in adults, is still a classic and is summarised here.

Lesions in the occipital region tend to impair visuo-perceptual and visuo-spatial functions and are reflected in confusions due to misreading numbers. Multiple digits are mistaken for discrete units, e.g. 89 read as 8, 9. Tasks involving analysis and synthesis cause difficulties and since visual imagery is implicated, patients with occipital lesions develop fewer useful calculating skills.

Some patients apparently experience uncommon difficulties in arithmetical calculations if the material is presented auditorily.

Some of the features of parietal lobe lesions, it is claimed, are difficulties in auditory discrimination, recall of digits and cross-model transfer from auditory stimulus to the written expression of the same. This view has not won general acceptance, partly because of insensitivity of tests used in studies and partly because efforts to ascribe auditory digit recognition to highly specific cortical regions are quite unconvincing.

It is claimed that one result of frontal lobe damage is weak abstract reasoning in mathematics, and that multiplication and division are more likely to be affected by lesions in this region than are addition and subtraction. The assumption that the former two operations involve more abstract reasoning skills than do addition and subtraction has little, if any, support. Clinicians have given much attention and speculation to the effects of damage to the parietal lobe. Among the functions affected, it is claimed, are calculating skills. Acalculia is reported to result from lesions of the angular gyrus. Fifty years ago the German neurologist Gerstmann (1924) described a complex of four symptoms in which right-left disorientation, finger agnosia and deficiencies in writing and counting resulted from left parietal lesions. Evidence for this claim has been disputed by Benton *et al.* (1951), who criticised the so-called supportive data offered by Strauss and Werner (1938) and Werner and Carrison (1942).

Kinsbourne and Warrington (1962 and 1963) on the other hand, claim that impairments in serial orderings (items arranged in definite sequence) were implicated in spelling, finger recognition, calculation and right-left orientation, and that constructional disorders were signs of development delays. In the absence of motor paralysis, a failure to carry out motor operations, such as block-building or copying a pattern, under visual guidance and monitoring, might be due to an inability to put elements together as a whole. In other words, a constructional disorder might not be a single dysfunction but a disturbance of several related functions, including spatial manipulative ability.

Conclusion

Arithmetic is a highly sophisticated skill and is based on hierarchically organised sub-skills rather than a single underlying ability. Calculation depends upon the efficient functioning of several processes including sensory, perceptual, motor, intellectual and social factors. The lack of any relevant skill, or delay in its development in both normal and handicapped children will set limits to arithmetical attainment. The role, therefore, of the teacher is to identify the developmental stage reached by a particular child, to specify the nature of the learning task and to set the educational scene, in order to exploit a child's existing skills and to generate new competencies.

SECTION 4: THE ORGANISATION OF EDUCATION

The last section discusses the philosophy behind attempts to educate handicapped children, briefly traces the history of such education and describes the present provision for this, particularly in England and Wales. The authors have included their own comments on the administrative situation at the time of writing.

A description is given of a special method originating in Hungary of educating severely physically handicapped children. This incorporates many of the ideas discussed earlier in the book. Finally, a chapter is included describing briefly the situation in the USA, followed by a discussion of various influential American educationalists and psychologists.

10 THE DEVELOPMENT OF EDUCATION FOR THE HANDICAPPED

Until the eighteenth century people who would now be referred to as 'handicapped' were regarded as some of nature's mistakes and were left to the care of hospital or church. In the late eighteenth century, however, from interest in the earlier work of the English philosopher Locke, a kind of intellectual curiosity about the handicapped was aroused. In his *Essay Concerning Human Understanding*, Locke put forward the view that the mind possessed no innate ideas and that knowledge was derived through the senses. Locke argued that the way ideas were formed was essentially an inductive one, and that the process of learning was by observation and experiment, and through the application of stimuli to the senses.

In the middle of the eighteenth century the philosopher, writer and educationalist, Jean Jacques Rousseau stressed the curiosity of the individual child as the source of learning, and prompted a new awareness of the child as a subject for scientific and intellectual study. Rousseau maintained that education should be based on the nature of the child, not on the requirements of an artificial society.

The influence of both these men was seen in the work of a French ear specialist, Jean-Marc Gaspard Itard (1775-1838) with a severely handicapped child, Victor, and this pioneering study marked a growth in the educational treatment, as opposed to the custodial care, of the handicapped. The intellectual curiosity of medical practitioners was presented with a challenge, hitherto unrecognised, and a tradition established from Itard can be seen in the individual studies, practice and research of doctors, teachers, educational administrators and educational psychologists.

Itard made a detailed study of Victor, 'the Wild Boy of Aveyron', and presented his findings to the French Academy in 1801 and 1806. The boy, a wild, deaf and dumb 'idiot' was discovered at about eleven years of age, in the forests of Aveyron, incapable of all but the most primitive of animal responses. He had lived on acorns and berries and had been unexposed to any form of human society. Itard took him into his care and began to train him systematically, using a technique of reward and punishment and of sensory stimulation. He attempted to socialise Victor, extend his concepts and ideas, and his awareness of people and events. He taught him language and gave him physical exercise, with the result that 'the biting, scratching boy' began to make some use of his senses, could remember, speak, write and count, though he could never be termed 'normal' as Itard had hoped he would.

The French Academy commented:

> The pamphlet of Monsieur Itard contains the exposition of a series of extremely singular and interesting phenomena, and fine judicious observations, and presents a combination of highly instructive processes, capable of furnishing science with new data, the knowledge of which cannot but be extremly useful to all persons engaged in the teaching of youth.

The important link which is made between science and education in these remarks, the notion that data could be accumulated which would be relevant in more than this one extraordinary case, the idea that the findings of a specialist could be of use to teachers, and above all the understanding that the skills of one discipline could interact with another were the origins of the twentieth-century multidisciplinary concern for the handicapped. The handicapped were elevated from their inferior position of a minority group to one of increased importance.

In Britain the practice of caring for rather than educating the handicapped had deep roots. Religious and charitable bodies predominated and established institutions and in some cases, schools. A tradition of doing things cheaply prevailed, generated by the Poor Law, together with the notion that the poor and the handicapped were so by virtue of their inherent wickedness. Men with noble intentions, like Thomas Cranfield the reformed dissolute soldier, John Pounds the crippled shipwright and the young medical student Thomas Barnado, attempted the redemption of delinquent and physically ill children who had been sold in pledge to their employers, and took these seven year-old waifs from sixteen-hour days in tobacco or pin-making factories into cramped airless classrooms where instruction in Christianity and 'the three Rs' for equally long hours was the order of the day. These 'Ragged Schools' and the notorious private schools at which Dickens directed his pen in *Nicholas Nickleby* were the educational norms for the poor and the unfortunate. The doctrines of 'self-help', of not pampering the children and of encouraging them to fend for themselves were taken to an extreme. Dickens said of his representation of these schools, 'Mr Squeers and his school are faint and feeble pictures of an existing reality purposely sub-

dued and kept down lest they should be deemed impossible.' Such
treatment inevitably associated the handicapped in general with a
tradition of 'second best'.

The industrial revolution and social matters, like the fight for the
right to vote at the beginning of the nineteenth century, occupied the
nation to the exclusion of any major developments in education. It was
not until 1870, with the advent of universal elementary education in
Britain, that children with physical and intellectual handicap,
malnutrition and debility began to be noticed within the ordinary
schools. It soon became apparent that there were some children who
differed from their fellows by virtue of poor sight or hearing, physical
or mental deformity, malnutrition and general ill health, and that the
ordinary schools could not cater for them. It was then that the notion
of education for the handicapped began, but only as an afterthought in
the wake of education for the normal child.

From 1895 onwards schools for what were termed 'defective'
children were established, these children being defined as having imper-
fections of body or phsyiognomy, abnormal neurological responses,
poor physical condition due to illness and poor nutrition, or mental
dullness. Other categories were 'imbeciles' (children who, due to mental
defect, were unable to be educated and become self-supporting) and
the 'feeble-minded' (children who were unable to receive ordinary
education but who were considered to be above imbecile standard).
Entry to these schools was decided by a physical examination made by
a doctor. As a rule conditions within the schools were poor, because of
overcrowding, lack of discipline and poorly paid staff employing inappropriate traditional teaching methods. This contrasts with Itard's
ideas which could apply equally well to handicapped and 'normal' children.

The neglect of the intellectually handicapped and the very cursory
attempts at educational provision for them at this stage need some
explanation. After all, the blind and the deaf had been receiving
education for over a century. The influence of Darwin's *Origin of the
Species,* propounding the theory of the survival of the fittest, may have
raised fears among the Victorians of the degeneration of the human
race through the 'unnatural' selection of its weak and deformed
members. Provision and care for these 'mistakes' in nature was interfering with and unbalancing the natural processes of human development. Indeed Darwin's cousin, Francis Galton, advocated the
segregation and sterilisation of the intellectually handicapped. His
equation of eminence with intelligence, and his refusal to consider the
environmental influences upon mental ability may be contrasted with

the attitude and practice of Itard. Galton's contemptuous and cruel descriptions of even the mildly handicapped as 'polluters of the noble stock of humanity, too silly to take part in general society but easily amused with some trivial, harmless occupation' was powerful discouragement for the already limited support for the education of such children. The long dark period of institutional and custodial care for the intellectually handicapped began with the ideas of Galton.

Abroad, however, the disciples of Itard, Seguin, Montessori and Binet were displaying a robust optimism about the modifiability of intellectual handicap that was finally to exert an impact upon the educational philosophy of that period. Seguin, for example, pleaded for 'the most rapid evaluation of the lowest and the poorest by all means and institutions, mostly by free institutions' and he advocated a social application of the principles of the Gospel in this matter. Binet protested 'against the limited pessimism' of the Darwinian and Malthusian attack on the perfectibility of human society. He established classes for the intellectually handicapped in which 'mental orthopaedics' in memory, logic, verbal attention and other related areas were offered and its effects systematically evaluated. Maria Montessori, herself a doctor, recognised that the needs of the handicapped with whom she worked were pedagogical, not medical. She devised her own system based on the writings of Itard and Seguin, trained her staff in these methods, and, encouraged by her success with the handicapped, applied her methods to ordinary children. The beginnings of an overlap in the methods of teaching for the handicapped and the ordinary child here represented another powerful move towards the integration as opposed to the segregation of the handicapped from the rest of the community. Indeed the innovations derived from work with this minority have given teachers working with ordinary children greater insights.

The twentieth century in Britain saw the establishment of what we now call 'special education', based initially on the German model. The English elementary schools still contained in the standard classes a ragbag of children, some of ordinary ability, some partially sighted, some 'imbeciles', some delicate or physically handicapped. In varying degrees these children truanted, misbehaved, were neglected and learnt very little. In Germany, however, the authorities had begun to provide for children who failed to progress after two years in the ordinary school. These children were seen by the head teachers of the ordinary and 'special' schools and by a doctor. The intellectually weak, who were poorly endowed in memory, perception and reason were admitted into the special school. The chronically disabled were not. In these schools, timetables were fairly free, much manual work was done and training for a useful activity was the main aim. In this country, Alfred Eichholz, an inspector appointed to work in the field of special education, drew up some important recommendations in 1899 concerning handicapped children, and anticipated the era of administrators and legislators in this field which culminated in the 1944 Education Act, a milestone in the history of education in England and Wales.

Eichholz defined three categories, the mentally deficient, the physically defective and the epileptic, and the physically and morally healthy who were nevertheless retarded. Three suggestions were made. The first group should attend schools in the country where farm work was the main activity and the possibility of doing harm was reduced. (The moral inferiority of the mentally deficient was still universally believed.) The second group should attend at a healthy residential site ,where good diet and medical supervision could be provided, and the last group should attend special day schools and return to the ordinary schools once their retardation had been overcome. Attendance at these schools would be from seven to fourteen, or sixteen if wished, and would be compulsory. The very mildly physically handicapped and epileptic were expected to attend ordinary schools. In the same year, a Bill in Parliament made the care of defective children necessary but not compulsory 'due to the difficulties and expenses of carrying out such care,' and by 1909,133 out of 328 local education authorities took up their responsibility.

This period in the early twentieth century saw the provision of school meals and the creation of the school health service. These were some results of examining the many unfit recruits called up for service in the Boer War. The examination revealed an undernourished population. It was not until 1944 that legislation specifically for the handicapped was drawn up. Local education authorities now had to educate all children in accordance with age, aptitude and ability, and any suffering from a disability of mind or body were to receive special education. Special education thus became a part of every local education authority's responsibility and not a separate requirement.

Then in 1944 the Education Act defined eleven categories of handicap, and provision was made for special education to take place outside special schools in separate classes in the ordinary schools. Children in long-term hospital care were also to be educated, and an attempt was made to suit education to the individual child's needs. It is significant that no major legislation has occurred since 1944, although a committee under the chairmanship of Mrs Warnock is currently studying the position of special education in its widest aspect. The immediate drawbacks of the 1944 Act as regards special education were the disruptive effects upon a child's education that moving between ordinary and special schools entails, the frequent mis-categorisation of children, insufficient provision by ordinary schools for special classes alongside ordinary classes, a still predominantly medical rather than educational reason for referral to special schools, and insufficient after-care for the special-school-leaver. These issues among others have occupied administrators and educationalists in the last few decades.

It is now being argued that the categories of handicap laid down by the 1944 Act need altering, and that a wider category, based on a learning disorder rather than a medical definition, should be adopted. Children suffering from a variety of handicaps which require a common educational treatment would then be grouped together. The HMSO pamphlet published in 1954 may be compared in its definition of handicaps with Younghusband *et.al.,* (1970) whose suggestions are significantly different.

HMSO	*Younghusband*
Blind	Visual handicap
Deaf	Hearing impairment
Educationally subnormal	Intellectual handicap
Maladjusted	Emotional handicap
Physically handicapped	Physical handicap
Speech defective	Speech and language disorder
Partially sighted	Specific learning disorder
Partially hearing	Severe personality disorder
Epileptic	Severe environmental handicap
Delicate	Severe multiple handicap

The reformation of categories is not just the changing of labels that it appears to be at first sight. It involves the rethinking of the special educational needs of the children involved. Suggestions such as these also help teachers to escape from the excessive specialisation resulting from training courses primarily devoted to one handicap. Evidence has shown that there is considerable overlap between handicaps; for example, over half of the cerebral palsied children have IQs below seventy; there is considerable overlap between educational subnormality and maladjustment, and the survey carried out on the school population of the Isle of Wight (Rutter *et al.,* 1970) indicates that one in four children with a handicap have additional handicaps. All practising teachers, doctors and educational psychologists will testify to the difficulties of categorising the handicapped children with whom they work under one single disorder.

The advent of comprehensive education, as an ideal and a working reality, in this country has not only the problem of independent schools yet to face, but also the problem of special schools. It appears less and less easy to justify separate educational systems for minorities of all kinds, the psychological disadvantages of segregation at any level seeming to outweigh any advantages. But much will have to be done to demonstrate the efficacy of integrating the handicapped with the rest of the school population, not only in terms of research, but also in the establishment of courses for teachers and administrators in colleges of education, institutes of education, and in the schools themselves. A great deal of work, planning and funds has gone towards the setting up of separate systems, and the devotees of the comprehensive approach will have to justify their position before changes on a large scale are made. Rutter *et al.* (ibid.) refer to the implications for services that their findings provide, and make practical recommendations. For example,'to establish new services on an experimental basis is much easier than to attempt to modify for experimental purposes long established services running on traditional lines'. They are in no doubt, though, as to the importance of research and experiment in relation to provision.

The future, to which this present work can only refer to speculatively, must be based upon experiment and research.

Social planning is an illusion without adequate facts; and the adequacy of services mere speculation without evaluation. Nor is it sufficient for research to be done spasmodically however good it be. It must be a continuing process, accepted as a familiar and permanent feature of any department or agency concerned with social provision (Seebohm Report).

11 THE EDUCATIONAL SERVICES IN ENGLAND AND WALES

In England and Wales special education is a part of the whole educational system and comes under the auspices of the Department of Education and Science. Individual local education authorities at county or county borough level run the services for their own areas by means of an elected council of members and appointed education officers. Finances are supplied from the local rates and from government grants provided for the purpose.

Within each local authority there exist a variety of schools providing special education. There are schools maintained by the local authority, and independent schools which are registered and inspected by the local authority. Independent schools may be in the charge of a charity or charities such as the Spastics Society. Local education authorities may pay fees for handicapped children in independent special schools. The task of every local authority, as defined in the 1944 Education Act, is to discover all those children in need of special education and to provide such education for them. The local education authority must also advise parents on their children's education, ensuring satisfactory school placement.

In the pre-school years, nursery schooling may be available. Later, the education of these children may take place within an ordinary school, in a day or a boarding special school, in a special class within an ordinary school, at home, in a hospital school, in a remedial centre, a training centre or a special care unit. After school age, handicapped young people may be educated in a sheltered workshop, an adult training centre, or a special college for further or higher education. Some cope in normal colleges.

Entry into special schools is by means of a medical examination, and children are recommended for special education by general practitioners or from infant welfare clinics or from hospitals or by a school medical officer. Educational psychologists are also involved in the assessment of children. Normally parents must give their consent. Although there are provisions in the 1944 Education Act for compulsory placement, this is seldom invoked. Approximately 1 per cent of the child population has special education.

The 1944 Education Act defines the categories of children for whom special education is to be provided as: the blind, the partially sighted, the deaf, the partially hearing, the educationally subnormal, the epileptic, the maladjusted, the physically handicapped, those with speech defects, and the delicate. Unfortunately, the provision of special schooling designed to cater for one main type of handicap may not serve the interests of a child physically, educationally or emotionally.

The handicaps from which any one child may suffer could include several of the following disabilities in various degrees of seriousness, especially if he has motor and neurological impairments. He may be mentally retarded, have convulsions, visual or hearing defects, speech defects or nutritional difficulties. He may have poor concentration; he may suffer from psychiatric disorders and have laterality difficulties. He may also have restricted use of some of his limbs and be limited in his movement generally. Incontinence may add to his problems.

One of the disadvantages of categorisation in terms of specific handicaps is that it inevitably means labelling by what is deficient in a child, instead of placing the emphasis on the assets of the handicapped child. If properly trained and fostered these assets are the most likely to help him lead a fulfilled life. Enlightened local education authorities may take this approach but it is not universally implemented.

A short summary of the types of school provided by the education authorities follows. The definitions of handicap are taken from the Handicapped Pupil and Special School Regulations, 1959, and the Amending Regulations, 1962.

Schools for the Educationally Subnormal

These schools are for 'pupils who, by reason of limited ability or other conditions resulting in educational retardation, require some specialised form of education wholly or partly in substitution for the education normally given in ordinary schools.' Pupils may be suffering from additional minor defects such as poor vision, hearing or speech. There are both day and residential schools for the educationally subnormal, usually with no more than a hundred and fifty or so pupils, in classes not exceeding twenty in number. Children are assessed at about eight or nine years of age and those of 50 − 70 IQ are considered to be educationally subnormal (moderate). In North America and Australia such children are classified as 'educable mildly retarded'. Depending upon their development, children may attend these schools for the whole of their school life or for a few years only.

Schools for the Physically Handicapped

Physically handicapped children are defined as 'pupils not suffering solely from a defect of sight or hearing who by reasons of disease or crippling defect cannot without detriment to their health or educational development, be satisfactorily educated under the normal regime of ordinary schools'. The range of children in these schools includes those with cerebral palsy, spina bifida, hydrocephalus and muscular dystrophy. Also attending schools for the physically handicapped are those suffering from asthma, Still's disease (juvenile rheumatoid arthritis – often now referred to as 'arthritis in children') or poliomyelitis, or from congenital conditions such as haemophilia, heart deformities and abnormalities caused by thalidomide. The children's IQs may range from approximately 60 to 130. Alternative provision for these children may be home tuition or facilities provided by a voluntary organisation, while a few authorities have special classes or units or tuition facilities in a normal school. Again school and class size is small, the maximum class size being twenty. Only a few of these children return to ordinary schools. Teachers in schools for the physically handicapped have to co-ordinate their work with specialists who deal with the physical needs of the children (e.g. physiotherapists, doctors and speech therapists).

Schools for the Maladjusted

'Pupils who show evidence of emotional instability or psychological disturbance and require special educational treatment in order to effect their personal, social or educational readjustment' are classified as maladjusted. They may be educated in day or residential schools according to their needs, and in classes of no more than fifteen children. School size is usually fifty pupils. Many local authorities do not have facilities for the maladjusted, and consequently these children may be wrongly placed elsewhere.

Schools for the Epileptic

Epileptic children are defined as 'pupils who by reason of epilepsy cannot be educated under the normal regime of ordinary schools without detriment to themselves or other pupils'. The kinds of epilepsy which occur include major epilepsy, in which there may be loss of consciousness, minor epilepsy, which creates a dizzy confused state, and *petit mal* in which there is a temporary 'switching off'. The side-effects of some of the drugs used to control fits may be seen in the moods and behaviour of these children and affect their learning ability. Classes do not exceed twenty in number.

Schools for the Deaf

Pupils in these schools are defined as those 'with impaired hearing who require education by methods suitable for pupils with little or no naturally acquired speech or language'. The catchment area for these schools is large, the class numbers no more than ten, and schooling may be day or residential.

Schools for the Partially Hearing

These children are defined as 'pupils with impaired hearing whose development of speech and language, even if retarded, is following a normal pattern, and who require for their education special arrangements or facilities though not necessarily all the educational methods used for deaf pupils'. Again class numbers do not exceed ten. Some partially hearing pupils are now being taught in special classes in ordinary schools, or in units on the same site as normal schools.

Schools for the Blind

The blind are defined as 'pupils who have no sight or whose sight is or is likely to become so defective that they require education by methods not involving the use of sight'. The blind are normally educated in residential schools in classes not exceeding fifteen in number. In at least one authority in England children registered as blind are educated with special facilities with children in normal schools.

Schools for the Partially Sighted

'Pupils who by reason of defective vision cannot follow the normal regime of ordinary schools without detriment to their sight or to their educational development, but can be educated by special methods involving the use of sight' are known as 'partially sighted'. They attend day or boarding schools or special units in normal schools.

Schools for Children Suffering from Speech Defects

These children are defined as 'pupils who on account of defect or lack of speech not due to deafness require special educational treatment'. There are in fact very few schools provided for these children and the majority of such children receive speech therapy either at school or in a clinic. Their disabilities may include aphasia (the delayed acquisition of spoken language), stammering, faulty articulation, the effects of cleft palate, and the effects of conditions such as autism and schizophrenia.

Schools for Delicate Children

These children are defined as 'pupils not falling under any other category in this regulation, who by reason of impaired physical condition need a change of environment or cannot, without risk to their health or educational development, be educated under the normal regime of ordinary shcools'. The commonest ailments of these children are bronchitis, asthma, general debility; children with mild epilepsy or diabetes are also included. Their stay in the special school is intended to be for temporary help, though some do remain throughout their school lives. Classes are officially no more than thirty in number. In these schools the number of children who have emotional and social difficulties which affect their educational development is increasing.

Schools for Severely Subnormal Children

Since 1971 schools for the severely subnormal have become the responsibility of local education authorities instead of the health authorities. These schools may be day or residential establishments. The children may have gross or multiple physical handicaps, have Down's Syndrome, or be autistic or psychotic. Special care units also exist for the totally incapable. There are also schools designed for one specific disability such as cerebral palsy, spina bifida, autism or dyslexia, and education authorities also provide a variety of services at home, in hospitals, special classes within ordinary schools and at remedial centres.

Home Tuition

Home tuition is available for children (a) who are convalescing after hospital treatment, (b) who are severely handicapped, (c) who, being maladjusted, are unable to be separated from their parents or who fear school, (d) whose classification is doubtful or who are awaiting special school places or admission to hospital, and (e) whose parents have refused places for them in special schools. The school medical officer decides about home tuition. The children may receive up to five sessions a week.

Hospital Schools

These cater for many different types of child; most have conditions which necessitate a lengthy stay in hospital. The doctor decides if a child should have teaching and the work of the teachers is co-ordinated with that of the medical specialists involved. The child's ordinary school is consulted where this is possible. Children may be taught in the wards of the hospital or in special classrooms set aside for the purpose or even in separate buildings. The schools are maintained by the local education authority, not by the hospital authority.

Special Classes in Ordinary Schools

These 'progress' or 'remedial' classes set within ordinary primary or secondary schools may contain children who are classified as backward (unable to do the work commonly done by children of their age), retarded (those whose educational attainments fall short of their estimated potential by two years) or those with behavioural problems. The classes may cater for all aspects of these children's education, or they may exist for the teaching of one particular subject. Selection of pupils for the classes is a matter for each individual school. 'Opportunity' classes serve the needs of an area.

Remedial Services

These services exist to provide temporary help for individual children either at remedial centres or through the work of peripatetic remedial teachers who are based at the centres and who visit schools in a particular area. The centres are usually run by educational psychologists and each is manned by a number of teachers.

Pre-school Facilities

The medical examination and the assessment of the development in the young infant now provided at welfare clinics (see Chapter 3) should help to recognise children likely to have educational problems later as well as diagnosing those with obvious handicaps. The findings of the Isle of Wight survey (Rutter, Tizard and Whitmore, 1970) however, suggest that medical examination either at school or in the pre-school years needs to be reconsidered in terms of content and procedure, in order to discard elements which are of little use in detecting possible difficulties and to include those that would be very useful. Furthermore, attention to detail in the procedure, standardisation of the examination, and improvements in the skill of examiners would greatly increase the accuracy and value of the examination.

Sheridan (1973) has argued for a variety of services in the first five years of the handicapped child's life. These include the early identification of handicap through the channels of developmental screening at infant welfare clinics, the keeping of an 'at risk' register at such clinics, which would contain information of all those children who appear to be liable to handicap, and the continued services of a single paediatrician as the child's doctor, with full access to the child and his records. She also recommends continued diagnostic observation of the child throughout illness or handicap, and the setting up of centres where handicapped children can be seen regularly and diagnoses altered or revised. Some local education authorities already provide some of these facilities. Nevertheless, the parents whose children were included in the Younghusband report (1970) frequently voiced complaints as to the lack of advice, information and support from services in the early stage of their children's lives. Inefficient and unsympathetic responses from general practitioners and insufficient time for discussion and explanation of their children's conditions at the critical stages of diagnoses were mentioned particularly. In addition, delays in diagnosis, which made the acceptance of the handicap harder for the family, and the lack of expert knowledge on the part of the general practitioners were referred to.

Pre-school provision for handicapped children is 'patchy'. Some authorities have nursery schools which handicapped children are encouraged to attend. Some physically handicapped schools have nursery departments for assessment, as well as education. The absence of pre-school education for the handicapped child is commented on by the authors of the Isle of Wight survey, who feel that the disadvantages in terms of certain experiences that these children do not have should be compensated for by specific nursery provision.

> Free play and an opportunity to experiment are valuable but on their own they are of little use to children who have not yet learned how to profit from such opportunities. . . Nursery schools must make deliberate efforts to provide 'specific' training which is appropriate in relation to the children's handicaps, whatever they are.

Which School?

Once a handicapped child reaches school age, it must be decided which type of school he should attend. Should he attend a regular school, or day or boarding special school? Many factors determine whether a child is happy and successful at school. Each factor will be discussed separately with regard to placement of a physically handicapped child.

1. Nature of Handicap and its Severity

It must be considered whether the child is able to cope with the physical environment of a regular school — stairs, distance of walking between rooms for lessons and moving about in the classroom. Many questions must be asked. Has the child physical ability to write and draw? If the child is in a wheelchair, are the corridors and doors wide enough for it? Are there ramps? Does a lift exist or can one be installed? Could a welfare assistant (the provision of which is much cheaper than special school fees) enable a child to overcome physical problems? How far would the purpose-built facilities of a special school, such as wide corridors, ramps, lifts, and modifications to equipment and furniture help the child? Are facilities such as physiotherapy and speech therapy readily available or will much valuable time be lost from school in procuring them, if they are available?

If a child has spina bifida and attendant incontinence, problems will arise in a regular school unless special provision is made for toileting, both by way of extra toilets and staffing to cope. If the nearest regular school is not suitable and a regular school further away may be, is it worthwhile transporting him there or if he has to be transported in any case, is it better to choose a special school?

2. Personality and Intelligence

If a child has a high IQ physical difficulties can often be overcome, unless he has personality problems. Many physically handicapped children, however, are, by the nature of their handicap, likely to encounter learning disabilities. It may well be that the small classes in a physically handicapped school will enable a child to make progress, whereas he will be unable to cope in a normal-sized class in a regular school, causing emotional difficulties later. Possibly, too, the child is anxious or withdrawn and will be unable to settle happily in a large regular school. It must be asked whether a child will be more harmed by the limited society and possible lack of physical, emotional and educational challenge in a school for the physically handicapped than by the 'rough and tumble' and pressures of a regular school. Consideration should also be given to the other members of the class, who may suffer if a child is disruptive or hyperactive, or takes up too much of a teacher's time.

3. Teachers

If a handicapped child is to be placed in a regular school, the teaching staff must be properly prepared, have access to specialist advice and possibly help from a peripatetic teacher. Special equipment, if necessary, should be available. Above all, the teacher should be happy about receiving the child in her class. Few teachers in regular schools have had training in teaching handicapped children. There are, however, many teachers in special schools who have not been specially trained. In-service training on a regular basis can help teachers enormously.

Special units within an ordinary school can provide the right balance between integrated and special schooling. Relationships between the head teacher, unit teacher and other school staff must be harmonious for this form of special education to be successful. Otherwise the children get the worst of both worlds — isolation and lack of full facilities.

If special schooling has been decided upon it may be necessary to decide between a day or residential school. A residential special school requires certain adjustments from a child. He has to make a break with the small community of home, family and friends, and move to the larger community of school. This may involve a move from town to country and distance may create difficulties for parents visiting, thus possibly leaving the child feeling isolated from his family. The child may, however, be less conscious of isolation at school because of the similarities between himself and the other children; this may not be the case at home in the available day school. The full-time specialist care available in the residential school can give much-needed relief to the parents and family of, for example, a maladjusted physically handicapped child. The previously strained relationships within the family may eventually improve. However, the somewhat limited society of the residential school may provide difficulties in adjustment within the normal community after school. If weekly boarding is possible this may prove the solution as the family has relief in the week and the child has contact with his family at the weekend. In some cases, however, the constant adaptations necessary may prove unsettling for both child and family.

When he has left school, a handicapped young person, possibly after further or higher education, at some point seeks a job. This is probably the most difficult period of his life, especially in times of economic depression. He may be able to seek advice from a specialist Careers Officer. If the handicapped young person acquires a job he may not be able to keep up with his workmates or adapt to changes in working arrangements. Many handicapped school-leavers have little hope of employment in a fiercely competitive world. Possibly schools should be placing greater emphasis on encouraging independence and leisure activities so that in a rapidly changing world a young person is less frustrated at his failure to reach unobtainable goals and more prepared to look after himself physically and occupy himself mentally.

12 THE EDUCATION OF EXCEPTIONAL CHILDREN IN THE UNITED STATES

In the USA, children who, in Britain, are usually referred to as 'handicapped' are called 'exceptional', a term which includes gifted children. An exceptional child is defined by Kirk as 'that child who deviates from the average or normal child in mental, physical or social characteristics to such an extent that he requires a modification of school practices or special educational services in order to develop to his maximum capacity'. This, however, is not a legal definition like the categories of handicapped children defined by the Act of 1944 in Britain.

The relationship between local, state and federal powers in educational matters must be understood before one can appreciate the diversity of American special education from state to state and the role which parents have played and are playing in the development of this special education. Variations occur not only between state and state but also between different localities in the same state. Generalisations cannot be made for the country as a whole except for certain basic federal principles.

In 1642 the governing influences of the Massachusetts Bay Company announced that each of its towns should select men to be responsible for seeing that members of the company were able to read and understand religion and the capital laws. In a few of these towns free schools were built and funds collected for the salaries of the schoolmasters, thereby establishing an historical precedent of local control in education. This local responsibility was well established by the time the Federal Constituion was adopted and the separate states then, as now, reserved the power to control the education of its young people.

Each state, through its constitution and/or laws, lays down the powers of local government agencies. Each local educational agency then enforces those special powers and other powers necessitated by them. The federal government cannot usurp the responsibility of the state for educational matters, although it can withhold federal funds until a state has met certain minimum federal standards.

It was not until 1867 that a federal Office of Education was established, and even then its function was limited to collecting information about and promoting the cause of education. The Office of Education has increased its powers over the years, slightly reducing local autonomy, and its functions now include 'the collection and dissemination of information, financial assistance and special studies and programmes. Although legally the states are still independent in educational matters they defy the federal government at the risk of being denied access to financial funds and assistance' (McCarthy and McCarthy, 1969).

For exceptional children the state provides a cost per child, per teacher or per classroom over and above the cost for each of those things for non-handicapped pupils. This is because special education inevitably demands a higher pupil-teacher ratio and is therefore more costly.

Before 1800 there was no provision for exceptional children in America; the mentally retarded were regarded, as they were elsewhere, as ineducable and were hidden away or left to their own devices (as was the 'village idiot' in Britain). Later in the century, inspired men and women, such as Horace Mann, Samuel Gridley Howe and Dorothea Dix, led the movement for establishing residential schools for the blind, the deaf, the retarded, the epileptic and the orphaned. A similar movement was then taking place in Europe. These schools offered training but the 'care' aspect was also important; often handicapped people spent their lives in these institutions. As early as 1871, however, Samuel Gridley Howe envisaged the decline of the use of residential schools and a trend towards integrating exceptional children into the 'common' schools with 'common' classmates.

In the early 1900s the movement towards special classes in the public schools began. (In this chapter the term 'public' school is used in its American sense as 'one financed by public funds'.) This was brought about largely by the representation of parents on public school boards and it was recognised that children should be educated as close to their homes as possible. The growth of towns, making the population less scattered, meant that special units could be more locally based. The number of public school programmes for exceptional children has increased intermittently since then. The most dramatic progress has been made regarding educational provision, research and legislation on behalf of exceptional children in the 1960s and early 1970s.

In the 1960s provision was made for graduate fellowships for training people for a career in teaching retarded children (Public Law 85-926) and funds for preparation of teachers of the deaf (Public Law 87-276). These two laws set the scene for great advances in legislation for the education of exceptional children. By 1968 two Public Laws, 88-164, Title III and, as amended, 89-750, Title VI, provided federal funds to educational institutions for training personnel in special education, financial assistance to those being trained and direct aid to states for their special educational programmes. Federal funds continued and were increased for research and experimentation. Many other Public Laws have provided funds which may be used for special education; for enterprises as diverse as libraries, captional films for the deaf and community health centres. Every Congress since the Eighty-fifth has passed laws benefiting exceptional children in some way.

Parental pressure groups were partly responsible for forcing this legislation to be passed. The success of the civil rights movement also had the side-effect of encouraging minorities, including those concerned with exceptional children, to push for amelioration of their legal position. The membership of societies working on behalf of exceptional children increased greatly in the 1960s. These had strong parental support. An example is the Council for Exceptional Children, one of the major professional associations. In 1963 membership was approximately 16,000. By April 1973 membership had grown to 48,000.

In 1970, President Nixon signed Public Law 91-230 – the Elementary and Secondary Education Acts 1969, The Education of the Handicapped Act – which was to combine new legislation and existing legislation within a single statute. This new law covered such things as administration at federal level, financial and advisory provision for the states, training personnel to work with exceptional children, research and special programmes for children with learning disabilities.

The next decade saw a tremendous increase in new provisions for exceptional children at state level. In some states the compulsory attendance laws had become the 'non-attendance laws' as the exclusion clauses were used against handicapped children. Examples are: 'children with bodily or mental conditions rendering attendance inadvisable' (in Alaska), exclusion may occur (in Nevada) when 'the child's physical or mental condition or attitude is such as to prevent or render inadvisable his attendance at school or his application to study'.

The legality of denying an education in public schools for some exceptional children has been challenged increasingly in the last few years. This challenge has been based on the Fourteenth Amendment to the US Constitution which guarantees to all the people equal protection of the laws. The first significant achievement in the right to education for handicapped children's movement was the outcome, in 1971, of the lawsuit brought against the Commonwealth of Pennsylvania by the Pennsylvania Association for Retarded Children and 13 mentally retarded children. The state had failed to provide access to a free public education for all retarded children. The court ruled in the plaintiffs' favour and, amongst other things, it was decided that by September 1972 all retarded children between the ages of 6 and 21 were to be provided with a publicly supported education. Similar lawsuits with comparable rulings followed in other states.

The PARC suit revealed the arbitrary way in which decisions about exclusions had been reached. Provisions were made for true representation of the parents or guardians in decisions about categorising the children. Provisions were also made for informing parents about the available services and alternative forms of education for exceptional children. Since 1974, parents have had the right of access to any school records kept on a child. Generally in the USA parents have been much more dominant in all educational matters than they have been in Britain. Parents have often been behind many of the advances in the provision for exceptional children. The British PTAs (Parent-Teacher Assocations) are much less powerful than their counterparts in the USA. It must be remembered, however, that a parallel growth on a smaller scale of societies for various groups and categories of handicapped children, largely originating from parents, took place in Britain in the 1960s, as it did in the USA.

Another area of controversy in recent times, in the USA as in Britain, is 'labelling' or putting exceptional children into categories. Similar arguments have been put forward against the existing categories in the USA as against those in Britain which have been discussed in Chapter 10. 'Labelling' cannot be altogether abolished but must be as accurate as possible. It has happened in the USA, as in Britain, that children from minority racial groups have been designated as mentally retarded when, in fact, their learning problems have stemmed from language and cultural differences rather than lower innate ability. Wrongful 'labelling' also has been the subject of litigation, as in the case of nine Mexican-American pupils aged 8 - 13, heard at the District Court of Northern California in January 1970. They successfully contested that they had been wrongly 'labelled' as mentally retarded, and the tests were considered to have been unfair. Revision of testing procedure for minority groups was ordered.

Parent groups seek federal recognition for the particular handicap in which they are interested because federal financial assistance may be given as categorical aid. This means that funds are earmarked for the education with a particular category of handicap. Federal aid can be given as general aid or categorical aid. Educators in special education tend to favour categorical aid as these funds will find their way directly to handicapped children without being syphoned off to regular education. On the other hand funds specified for one kind of handicap cannot be used for another, for example, funds for the mentally retarded cannot be used for the deaf or children with learning disabilities. There is a 'wastebasket' category in which handicaps not included in the primary categories (auditorily handicapped, visually handicapped, mentally retarded, physically handicapped) can be put. These minority groups have to compete with each other for the funds allotted to the 'wastebasket' category. It is therefore preferable to have a handicap recognised, hence the effort to put categories such as 'learning disabilities/behaviourally disordered' into a legal framework. In due course these problems will be sorted out with the vigour associated with reform in the USA.

Psychology and Philosophy

The early American educators were influenced by European thinkers, psychologists and educators. It was not long, however, before the USA made its own contribution and Europe was receiving ideas back from the USA. Development of easier and quick communication between the countries helped to make the exchange of ideas possible. A few of the developments pertaining to children with motor and neurological deficits will be discussed here.

British and American notions of intelligence developed along different lines. The British favoured the concept of 'g' or general intelligence and developed a hierarchical model of intelligence. The American notion, exemplified by Thurston and Cattell, was that different skills and aptitudes were not hierarchically organised from 'g' and could therefore be tested separately.

The British and Americans have held similarly divergent views of the concept of personality – the British having a hierarchical notion and the Americans a more separatist one, as is shown by the two personality tests (Eysenck, 1959 and Cattell, 1963). Mental testing and personality testing have flourished in the USA more than in any other country. Some of the more widely used tests have been mentioned in previous chapters. Binet's test of intelligence has been modified (Terman-Merrill, 1960) and other intelligence tests standardised (WISC, 1949). Tests have been developed for such other things as visual perception (Frostig,

1964, Bender Visual-Motor Gestalt 1962); auditory perception (Wepman, 1957) and motor development (Lincoln-Oseretsky, 1956). An important diagnostic test of faults in decoding, processing and encoding language (see 'Spelling') is the Illinois Test of Psycholinguistic Abilities (Kirk and McCarthy, 1968) which has undergone revision since it was first brought out. This test is used extensively in diagnosing faults in a child's language processing. Remedial measures are suggested according to the findings of the test.

The Frostig Developmental Test of Visual Perception aims at testing five areas of visual perception which are deemed crucial to pre-reading skills, viz. eye-motor co-ordination, figure-ground discrimination, constancy of shape, recognition and perception of position in space and spatial relationships. A programme has been devised to remedy weaknesses in these areas of visual perception (Frostig, 1964). Factor analytical studies have not upheld the claim that five areas are in fact tested by the Frostig Test. There is evidence to show that visual perception itself can be improved by the programme but not that this, on its own, helps poor readers. For improvement of reading, other skills need to be developed also, as we have discussed in other chapters.

The possibility of using a selection of the tests mentioned has helped teachers to diagnose weaknesses in their pupils' learning ability and to plan remedies for them.

Kephart's Contribution

Before he produced *The Slow Learner in the Classroom* (1961), Kephart had worked with Strauss and, indeed, many of his insights come from his earlier work. He is also strongly influenced by the theories of Piaget and Hebb. In his book, Kephart discusses children who are presenting learning difficulties and who need help to overcome them but who have no serious physical disability or obvious neurological damage. Kephart maintains that these children's problems stem from inefficiency in perceptual-motor skills. These perceptual-motor problems are mainly physical. They are often made worse, however, because children living in the modern environment are not required to develop the skills, such as eye-hand co-ordination, form perception and intersensory integration, which Kephart considers basic to academic learning. He has worked out ways of developing these skills. Kephart emphasises that it is necessary to develop basic skills in their natural order of sequence. He says, 'training is easier if it is begun with the most basic area of performance in which the child is weak.' A number of tests, which have not been standardised, are described. These detect deficiencies and are used to monitor progress in overcoming them.

Kephart stresses the effect of movement on perception and perception on higher thought processes. He also emphasises the part played by feed-back in perception and the interplay between motor learning and perceptual learning. It is only through exposure and practice that perceptual-motor skills develop. Such things as practice in writing and drawing on a chalkboard, walking along beams, balancing, playing with balls and tracing templates are used in his remedial programme. Music is used extensively to encourage listening skills, rhythm and co-ordinated movement. Intersensory integration in the form of auditory motor skills are developed by musical games.

Kephart discusses what he calls 'splinter' skills, which are skills that have developed in advance of more basic ones. These skills, therefore, are not generalised and are of little value. Kephart maintains that teaching skills which can be generalised is of paramount importance: teaching a specific task has to follow later. He therefore first concentrates on such things as broader aspects of body image' — knowledge of parts of the body, laterality and directionality.

We can see that many of Kephart's ideas have been discussed earlier in this book. In the USA classrooms have been set up to enable teachers to follow Kephart's programmes. In Britain Kephart's ideas have not systematically been put into practice on any large scale. Kephart has been criticised (Cratty, 1972) for his poor grounding in neuro-physiology and questionable motor assessment technique. His ideas have, however, influenced thinking in special education in the last decade and a half.

Grace Fernald*

Grace Fernald's kinaesthetic techniques for teaching children with visual and auditory disorders are well known to those working in special education. Fernald anticipated many current ideas with her insight into learning difficulties and with her methods of overcoming them. She believed that children should first read their own stories rather than those adults had written for them. (This approach has since been incorporated into reading schemes such as 'Breakthrough to Literacy'). She thought that the child's interests and ideas should dictate the content of his reading and writing. She also thought that continual success is essential not only for learning to read but also for other forms of learning because failure causes emotional stress which hinders progress.

*'Remedial Techniques in Basic School Subjects', 1943.

By Fernald's method, a teacher has first to find some means by which the pupil can be motivated and guided to writing words correctly. The child then reads a printed copy of his own words, and, finally, will read other material. We shall now describe the method in greater detail.

At first, a child chooses a word which is written in enlarged script on a card. The child then traces the word with his finger, enunciating it as he does so. He repeats this process until he is able to write the word as a whole unit, on his own, from memory. The card is then filed. The child then has to try to use the word in a story. At first his stories will consist of a few words only, but they increase in length over a period of time. In the next stage tracing is omitted and the child looks at the word, speaks it and then continues as before. Now the words are no longer in specially large script. Word cards are not used in the third stage. The child looks at the printed word, speaks it and writes it while saying it. At this stage the child shows a desire to read from books. He is allowed to read whatever he likes, and is told words he does not know. When he finishes reading a passage he 'goes over' new words and writes them down. All words are later revised.

In the fourth stage the child is taught to recognise new words from their similarity to words or parts of words he already knows. During this stage Fernald did not read to the children and she asked parents not to read to them either.

Fernald's ideas and methods, although still useful for a fresh approach in remedial teaching, have been incorporated into present-day regular teaching techniques. Her emphasis on success, interest and learning in small sequential steps incorporating motor activity is thoroughly in accordance with modern thinking and was a considerable contribution before many had begun seriously to consider learning disabilities.

Doman-Delacato

The Doman-Delacato approach is attracting considerable attention at present and so we have included a brief description and discussion of their theories. Delacato maintains that 'if the problem lies in the nervous system, we must treat the nervous system', and that ontogenic development reflects phylogenetic development. Basically, their theory is that normal human development parallels the evolution of the human race. They consider that this evolution goes from fish to amphibians, to 'land-animals', to primates, all with their developing types of movements, to end in man, who is capable of rational thought. Man's neural development parallels this evolutionary development from the beginning, when the baby is in the period of gestation, to the time a child reaches about eight years of age.

According to Delacato, neurological organisation takes place with the increase of myelinisation, starting at the spinal cord and working towards the cortex. The development is systematic and dependent upon each level being organised at the correct stage. The process ends with the organisation of the cortex with one hemisphere being dominant. According to this theory, abstract thinking, present only in humans, is dependent upon hemispheric dominance.

At birth the spinal cord and medulla are the most highly organised structures. At about four months (crawling stage), when the child is becoming mobile, he leaves the level of organisation paralleling that of the fish and enters that which parallels the amphibians. At six months neural organistion has reached the mid-brain — this brings him to the level paralleling 'land-animal'. He can now crawl: he has binaural hearing and binocular vision. Neural fibres associated with sight, sound, balance, posture and movement are linked. At this stage the child can move his opposite hand and leg simultaneously. At twelve months, organisation parallels that of the primates and the child can walk. The cortex is now organised. Finally, at about eight years, cerebral dominance is well established and the child is capable of abstract thought.

Doman and Delacato insist that children who do not go through these stages because of damage to their central nervous system have to be taken through them before they can progress normally. Such a child going for assessment is clinically examined and the point at which neural organisation has broken down is determined. Treatment is aimed at re-organising subsequent disorganised levels. For example, according to Delacato, if a child's neural organisation has reached the level of the medulla only and yet he has problems of movement although he is several months or years old, he would be programmed for organisation at the next level. This would mean making him use any reflex movements he has managed to develop, and any of which he is at the moment incapable are passively imposed on him by several adults in a 'patterning' programme. At the level of cortical organisation, in an effort to evolve dominance of one of the cerebral hemispheres, there is retraining of sleep patterns (considered important by Doman and Delacato). Then dominance, right or left, of foot, hand and eye is trained.

The neurological and theoretical views of Doman and Delacato have been severely criticised over the years. Although some improvements have been shown by patients treated by this method, critics argue that improvements of even severely handicapped children might be expected as a result of the intensive treatment given by the large number of adults required for this programme. Strictly controlled research is required to assess more accurately this and other methods of treating neurologically impaired children.

Skinner's Contribution

B.F. Skinner has made significant contributions to educational thinking by his work on conditioning techniques, namely operant conditioning, to which reference has been made in this book. This can best be explained by describing Skinner's famous experiments.

Skinner built a 'Skinner box' containing a lever which, when pushed, released a food pellet. A hungry rat was placed in the box and the rat by chance pressed the lever and so obtained food. Gradually the rat realised that food followed the lever-pressing and it pressed the lever when it wanted food. The formula is:

Stimulus (S)	Response (R)	Reinforcement
(desire for food)	(rat's pressing lever)	(food pellet)

This and similar procedures are called operant or instrumental conditioning, the rat's behaviour or response being operant or instrumental in obtaining reinforcement or food. This is essentially a learning procedure. The best results are obtained if the delay in reinforcement is small. Skinner showed that rats entering a correct goal box in a T-maze who were rewarded immediately performed better than those whose reward was delayed. Extinction occurs, i.e. the subject fails to respond, if reinforcement is discontinued. The rat will give up pressing the lever if there is no reinforcement, i.e. the food ceases to appear. However, spontaneous recovery or renewed response will be shown after there has been extinction, followed by a period of rest; a rat will respond anew with his lever.

Skinner found that rats can show discrimination in their response according to the stimulus. If food is presented in the Skinner box only when a light is on when the lever is pressed, rats learn to press the lever only then. Reinforcement can be made 'partial' and can be regulated by such means as fixed ratio (reinforcement every fixed number of trials) or fixed interval (reinforcement every fixed interval of time). Pigeons peck so hard at a disc to obtain food at a fixed ratio that their beaks become sore. It has also been shown that larger rewards result in greater learning.

Operant conditioning shows that secondary reinforcement is effective. This is any stimulus which reinforces because of its associations with an original reinforcement. For example, a rat in a Skinner box may be conditioned to respond with a tone followed by food. Gradually the tone and the food are withheld, resulting in extinction of the animal's response. After a time the rat will press the lever for the reinforcement of the tone, even if the food is withheld.

These animal experiments, demonstrating learning in its simplest form, have given insight to human learning. As a result of his work with animals Skinner developed linear programmes putting them into teaching machines. In linear programming material to be learnt is broken down into small sequential steps. Each step has to be mastered before the pupil proceeds to the next. As the steps are so small, re-inforcement (reward by means of obtaining the correct answer) is frequent and consequently learning is steady and fast. All kinds of developments and variations have followed from Skinner's work. Examples are branching programmes (whereby 'learning steps' are made larger than in linear programming and if one gives the wrong answer the learner is directed to a 'branch' which covers the point of difficulty in greater detail), graded work-books and word-cards. The aim for these teaching aids is to enable a child to work at his own pace and to free the teacher from routine work for work which needs personal and individual attention. The notion of continual success is especially important for exceptional children who may easily become discouraged. As many children who are handicapped miss schooling for reasons of health or treatment, means whereby they can work on their own are to be welcomed.

Skinner's work has had the general effect of emphasising to educators two main points, viz. the importance of positive reinforcement (i.e. reward in the form of success and constant praise for even small achievements) and the frequent necessity of 'breaking down' a learning task into small sequential steps. If a child is failing at a task it must be analysed into even smaller components, each of which the child can master. Many handicapped children fail because tasks demanded from them, although fairly easily mastered by unhandicapped children, are too great for the handicapped child without being analysed into a series of simpler tasks.

A side-effect of Skinner's work has been the development of behaviour modification, whereby a pupil's unacceptable social behaviour is altered to make it more compatible with that of his social environment, e.g. his class at school. This is done by making a careful study of:

1. the behaviour to be modified;
2. the reinforcement which the child considers to be positive;
3. the stimuli causing the unacceptable behaviour.

A programme is worked in which acceptable behaviour is suitably rewarded and unacceptable behaviour is ignored. This is a very simple exposition of a procedure which merits a fuller explanation than we have space for here. Critics of behaviour modification maintain that, although the symptoms of unacceptable behaviour are treated, its cause is not.

Special education in the USA is provided in residential special schools and in special classes at regular schools. Although it is difficult to make generalisations in so large and varied a country it is generally true to say that the trend is towards integrating, where possible, exceptional children into regular classes. Use is made of special resource rooms and specialist staff who are either on the school staff or are peripatetic. In recent years there has been great expansion in the number of training courses for teachers of exceptional children. Many more directors of special education have been appointed at local and state level to co-ordinate services and give advisory help. To enable children in hospital to receive an education, there are hospital schools and teachers attached to hospitals, as in Britain.

TESTS

Auditory Discrimination Test. Wepman Joseph, and M. Joseph, Language Research Associates, Chicago, 1958.

Bender Visual-Motor Gestalt Test for Children. Aileen Clawson, Western Psychological Services, Beverly Hills, California, 1962.

Marianne Frostig Developmental Test of Visual Perception. Marianne Frostig, D. Welty Lefever, John R.B. Whittlesey and Phyllis Maslow, Consulting Psychological Press, Palo Alto, California, 1964.

Illinois Test of Psycholinguistic Abilities (revised edition). Samuel A. Kirk, James J. McCarthy and Winifred D. Kirk, Univeristy of Illinois Press, Urbana, Illinois, 1968.

Lincoln Oseretsky Motor Development Scale. William Sloan, C.H. Stoelting Co., Chicago, 1956.

The Maudsley Personality Inventory. H.J. Eysenck, University of London Press, London, 1959.

The Sixteen Personality Factor Questionnaire (16 PF). R.B. Cattell, Institute for Personality and Ability Testing, Illinois, 19XX.

Standford-Binet Intelligence Scale. Revised IQ tables by Samuel R. Pinneau, Lewis M. Terman and Maud A. Merrill, Houghton Mifflin Co., Boston, Mass., 1960.

13 CONDUCTIVE EDUCATION

Here we give an account of a pedagogical method for teaching children with motor handicaps which differs from contemporary practices in a number of respects. It emphasises the development of functionally useful movements, to facilitate independence in feeding, dressing and personal/social skills, before formal academic learning is attempted. The children are encouraged to apply their skills and abilities to the utmost limit, but within the realistic bounds set by the 'conductor'. It appears that the theoretical insights gained from neurology, psychology and pedagogy have been skilfully incorporated within this system and effectively applied to promote learning in children with motor handicaps.

Professor Peto, in Budapest, worked out and established his own training scheme to help motor and neurologically impaired children. Peto called his scheme 'conductive education' and it is now practised in the state-owned Institute for Motor Disabled in Budapest. Most of the children who attend the Institute suffer from cerebral palsy, although children, and even adults, with other handicapping conditions, for example spina bifida and muscular dystrophy, attend also.

The basic principles of conductive education are set out below.

1. The Conductor

One of the most important principles of conductive education is that children must receive their education from as few people as possible. Girls straight from High School study for four years in the 'Conductors' College' which exists within the Institute. At the end of a rigorous training, consisting of six hours a day of theory and higher education and six hours of practical work with the children, the conductors are qualified to teach every aspect of a child's learning needs in a carefully structured system of total education. This is aimed at making a child physically and emotionally independent and integrated into normal society. The conductors work with parents' groups, training mother and child, with out-patients and with groups of residential or 'in-patients'. The conductors work with these allocated groups of in-patients in six-hour shifts, thereby ensuring that a staff with identical training and responsibility is with the children 24 hours a day, giving continuity of education.

168

1. Meal time at the Institute.

2. Child on a plinth learning to stretch forward in prone position.

3. Exercises on a plinth, using head and eye control.

4. Learning to stand with aid of a ladder-back chair.

5. Child learning to stretch upright.

6. Walking, using a chair as a support.

6

5

4

The conductors are highly trained and respected and work with every aspect of a child's development, ensuring that there is a transfer of learning from one activity to another. In the course of her work with children a conductor gives positive reinforcement only. She is not allowed to scold or rebuke or tell a child that his effort is poor or his movement is in any way bad. She can only praise and encourage. This approach is very similar to that of 'operant conditioning' – a technique devised by B.F. Skinner.

2. Group Work

At first a child and his mother attend the parents' school. Here the mother is taught how she should manage at home with such things as the child's feeding and dressing. 'The goal is to activate the child. The mother learns what task to set the child in order to make it co-operate with her' (Hari, personal communication). The mother returns periodically for check-ups and tasks are changed according to progress. At this early stage emphasis is placed not on movement but on encouraging responses in the child, for example, to his name and his mother's approach, and increasing his interest in his surroundings. He also learns 'to play and go on playing, building up his endurance' (Hari, personal communication).

After five or six months the child matures so that he can participate in group work within the frame of the 'parents' school. These groups work every other day for 1½-2 hours. The mother learns how to organise the entire daily programme for her child so that he becomes increasingly independent. In the Institute a child has only two pieces of furniture: a solidly-built chair without arms and a wooden slatted plinth on which he exercises and uses as a table. If a child becomes an in-patient he sleeps on the plinth also.

All occupations are kindergarten activities and lead to education. The goal is to attempt by visual and auditory stimulations to make the child react to verbal demands and consequently to learn activities leading to definite goals. These goals should be reached by play. One should not use abstract movements, but always set a goal. The group occupation is structured so that each game prepares for the development of self-help. In the beginning the children may feel insecure on the 'pot' because it is a new situation. To minimise the insecurity they must grasp a ladderback and the 'pot' may be of a larger size.

How precisely does the group work in the parents' school? First, activation by roll-call or song, then potting, hand-washing and eating. It is important that the children become noisy, lively and interested while they are eating. When they eat, they sit on small chairs in front of the plinth which is used as a table. The soles of the feet should be flat on the floor (or stool). The children eat the food they have brought. The mother is taught how she can make the child himself put the spoon, bread or mug to his mouth. One teaches the child to swallow when he drinks and slowly one proceeds to solid food, the child learning to chew. Swallowing and chewing prepares for speech. The mother must understand that using a bottle may delay speech development. After the meal comes standing, walking and movement. There must be purposeful movement, the movement having an aim. The playing finishes with going home.

The individual child is not, however, forced into an unacceptable stereotyped pattern of behaviour.

The common demands make it possible for different types of dysfunction to be grouped together. The programme is common to them all. One works for independence in feeding, toiletting and mobility. The individual difficulties are different and one must find the individual means to reach a goal. Those who cannot walk may creep or crawl or roll. (Some may have to learn to turn the body into prone position; others, the position of the head when crawling.) Every solution is temporarily acceptable. To reach the goal is the tool to further 'autofunction'. Some may temporarily have boots to prevent flexion of the knees. Others may have a raised heel to make the heel touch the ground. To be able to walk, a child must first learn to stand with support. A small ladderback is provided and a child learns to grasp and release it with his hands. He pushes it in front of him and stops at each step. He learns to let go for a second. Later he claps with his hands above his head, by which he obtains security in standing, and stretches the trunk (Hari, personal communication).

At this stage, the group work benefits the mothers almost more than the children. The mothers receive individual guidance in a relaxed atmosphere while they themselves are working with the children. Mothers become less anxious and learn to become responsible for their children's education themselves instead of relying on specialists. They can compare their children's progress with that of other children in the group and share the problems common to other mothers of similarly handicapped children.

If a child progresses well in the parent group he will transfer to the out-patient group where he will work two to six hours a day in a group without the mother. The children attend as day patients. Some children become 'autofunctioning' as out-patients; others may have to become in-patients. The most intense Conductive Education is carried out on an in-patient basis (Hari, personal communication).

These in-patients are placed in groups according to their diagnoses and speed of activity. There is a range of ages in each group providing a type of family situation and necessitating some reassortment for school work. The children benefit from being in a group as they can learn from and interact with each other instead of being 'adult dominated'. The conductor can study a child unobtrusively in a social setting. The group momentum can influence a child who is resisting. Not least, a child cannot be too dependent on the conductor in a group of fifteen or more children. The group also provides security; in his group a child can learn to cope with and control his emotions, knowing that he is part of a stable situation. A child also learns how to give and take; he can help others as others help him in giving advice or assistance in overcoming a problem of movement or posture.

3. The Programme

Daily and weekly time-tables are made to fit into a definite plan by which to accomplish a definite objective. The schedule extends to every aspect of life; to movement, to seeing and hearing, speech and writing, singing, playing percussion instruments, kindergarten and school, arts and crafts, use of tools and finally work in a shop or factory.

Parnwell (1971) summarises the programme:

At the same time that the children are learning the elements of physical control through active exercises in lying, sitting and standing and detailed hand exercises, they are putting into practice their increasing control and body awareness in active situations of every-day life. They do not wait to achieve a normal pattern of movement before using it in function; they concentrate on function from the very beginning, and so they are psychologically and emotionally prepared for functional independence as it becomes a physical possibility. The constant background of training ensures a gradual progression towards normality of motor functioning within this active and practical framework of living.

Exercises, carefully graded, are performed systematically with 'rhythmic intention' (q.v.). 'There is no place for improvisation in the conductive process. The progressive movement problems always have to be based on already existing results. Improvisations disregarding already established laws are senseless; they prevent progress' (Hari, personal communication).

4. Rhythmic Intention

'Rhythmic intention' is a very important part of conductive education. Briefly, it involves reciting aloud all together, with the conductor, the action or movement before it is done and as it is done. The group might then sustain a position and count aloud rhythmically. For example, a child might say, 'I raise my hand. I stretch my fingers. I place my hand on the plinth. One, two, three, four, five.' In the case of speech defects, substitutions are found for the usual words. Peto believed that the order that would be developed in the brain by the work focused on speech and hand dexterity would be reflected in the performance of the whole body. Whether this is true or not, observers have remarked on the usefulness of the hands of children at the Institute and the fact that there is little or no gap, as is often the case in Britain, between physiotherapy and function.

5. After-Care

A daily timetable of the most important activities is compiled for the period following discharge and given to each patient. Regular 'follow-ups' are made at the home, in school or the place of work. Social activities are also included in the programme, such as singing, music, drama, sports and dancing, enabling a patient to participate in normal social life on discharge.

Psychological Basis for Conductive Education

Professor Peto based his form of education on sound psychological and neuropsychological principles. These are described below.

Motivation

Motivation has a firm neurological basis. The brain cortex of a motivated learner will set the reticular formation of the brain so that more information is received. Conductive education concentrates from the beginning on getting a child motivated as has been described. 'Children only cry if an activity is forced on them' (Hari, personal communication).

Conceptualising Techniques

The three types of conceptualising techniques, i.e. imagery (thinking about the movements necessary for performance), directed mental practice (directing the thinking of the performer through specific instruction) and verbalisation techniques (the performer describes movements or associated feelings through the spoken or written word) are used in conductive education. As we have seen, these three techniques have proven value in improving motor skills.

Feedback

The learner of a motor skill can draw upon two types of feedback: internal feedback, which is related to kinaesthesis, and external feedback, which is concerned with knowledge of results. Movements of any kind provide internal feedback. Additional information which may be provided following the performance of a skill is referred to as 'knowledge of results'. Conductive education provides both internal feedback via the carefully devised exercises and knowledge of results, which is provided by the conductor. The exercises are often repeated, providing practice.

This is an important feature of the training programme — children love repeating the exercises and feel confident when rehearsing a newly learned skill like the ability to stand, or sit up. As Kay (1970) argues — There is a 'joy of repetition':

> In his strange world a child comes to love repeatable happenings; by repetition he begins to control the world around him. Eventually he will acquire such control that he will seek out the spice of life — variety — but for the present he has too much of it and so he pleads for the familiar story with its known ending, or the practised game which he has mastered and where he can demonstrate his proficiency. It is not surprising, therefore, that where so much is unknown a child creates its own redundancy by its love of repetition. We have to build on practised units of behaviour.

In many instances, for such children, the practice of a motor skill is interrupted, either by time between sessions, weekends, or breaks in concentration caused by various inappropriate stimuli in the environment. By the use of an integrated programme taught by trained conductors, conductive education gives the maximum opportunity for retention of learned motor skills.

Summary

The systematic programme laid down for conductive education applies throughout the waking period of the children, and this is held as one of the cardinal features of the method. As a result, the range of activities (movement patterns) performed by the children becomes severely restricted and largely predictable. Instead of having a wide range of movements, many of which are inadequately and incompletely executed, the sheer repetitive character of the teaching creates a structured framework in which there is a chance for frequent reinforcements of every aspect of motor training. In terms of simple conditioning theories, there is a greatly facilitated reinforcement of common elements of similar motor patterns and a markedly reduced interference of established movement patterns by random, chance interruptions. This in itself should enhance the motor development of children with severely handicapped motor control.

A second, and probably equally important, aspect is that as a result of the speech accompaniments the children are offered a reinforcing schedule for the movements before these are undertaken, i.e. a set towards the movements develops, is reinforced by the planned utterances and maintained due to the rhythmic and practised speech content. A different feature which is associated with this, which is applicable to many spastic children and to athetoid children in particular, is that the problems of performing two movements simultaneously are enormously greater than those of performing one at a time. By obliging the children to speak at the same time as they are executing other movements, this is achieved, and over-practised to a considerable degree. This means that the total movement pattern is broken down into its constituent elements, and that the systematic and practised element is increased still further. In summary, the Peto method of conductive education offers a means for continuous and frequent reinforcement on one hand, and for the elimination of extra, interfering movements on the other.

Conductive education seems to be very effective in Hungary. There are, however, no published results of controlled experiments to evaluate the method scientifically. In Britain there have been a few attempts to introduce conductive education. Again, there has to date been no scientific appraisal of their effectiveness. At present there is a lack of trained conductors outside Hungary, although training facilities are being set up in one school in Britain.

POSTSCRIPT

The authors have attempted to explain and discuss four main aspects of motor and neurological disabilities in children, viz. medical, psychological, pedagogical and educational, briefly and simply, for the educated and interested non-specialist involved in the care and education of physically handicapped children. We have described philosophical and educational theories and medical and psychological experiments which, though not perhaps immediately apparent in their relevance to the education of motor and neurologically handicapped children, have much to offer in this respect. We have also referred to teaching practices which are based on sound psychological principles.

We have tried to indicate where difficulties may arise when a child's normal reaction to his environment is incomplete, as it is with a motor-impaired and neurologically disordered child. It is hoped that the reader will have been prompted and encouraged to think anew upon the predicament of the children for whose benefit this book has been written.

GLOSSARY

Abduction: movements of the limbs towards the midline of the body.

Agnosia: inability to recognise objects, events, sounds, etc., even though the sense organ is not basically defective. A subject receives information but is unable to comprehend or interpret it. Usually a specific rather than general agnosia as in:

  auditory agnosia: inability to differentiate between various common sounds.

  form agnosia: form discrimination difficulty, for example geometric forms.

  tactile agnosia: inability to recognise common objects by touch alone.

  visual agnosia: difficulty in recognition of objects or people, even though they should be easily recognised (old acquaintances, etc.).

Agraphia: inability to relate kinaesthetic pattern (required motor movements) to visual image of a word or letter.

Akinetic seizure: an attack in which there is absence or loss of the power of voluntary movement.

Alimentary system: the system of the body relating to the provision of food or nourishment, *the digestive system.*

Alimentary tract: digestive pathway.

Amnesia: the partial or total loss of memory for past experiences (long-term memory). The memories lost in amnesia have not been completely destroyed for the forgotten events may again be remembered without relearning when the person recovers from his amnesia.

Anencephaly: the absence of the brain.

Anoxia: deficiency in oxygen carried by the bloodstream, resulting in lack of available oxygen to any particular part of the body so affected.

Antagonistic muscles: muscles arranged in pairs so that when one contracts, the other stretches, e.g. the biceps and triceps muscles of the upper arm (cf. reciprocal innervation).

Aphasia: inability to perform purposeful movements although there is no muscular or sensory loss or disturbance.

Arnold-Chiari malformation: a specific malformation of the cerebellum frequently associated with spina bifida.

Arthrogryposis multiplex congenita: generalised lack of musculature or muscle development from birth, with contraction or crooking of the joints.

Arthritis: from Greek *arthron* – joint and *itis* – inflammation – literally 'an inflamed joint'. Although arthritis is popularly used nowadays to describe any ache or pain in the entire skeleton; it should be reserved for cases of true joint involvement.

Association areas: areas of the cerebral hemisphere other than the projection areas. Because their function is unknown, it is assumed that these areas serve an integrative ('association') function.

Associated movements: unintentional movements accompanying motor functions.

Astereognosis: inability to recognise objects by feel and touch.

Asthma: a disease due to spasmodic contraction of the bronchi because of allergies or other irritations, resulting in wheezing, coughing and paroxysmal panting.

Ataxia: defective muscular co-ordination, sometimes due to lesions in the cerebellum, pons, or medulla oblongata.

Athetosis: a disorder, usually due to brain lesion, marked by slow, sinuous, and continual change of position of the fingers, toes, hands and other parts of the body.

Atonia: poor or insufficient muscle tone.

Basal ganglia: the optic thalami and corpora striata.

Brain damage: any actual structural (tissue) damage due to any cause or causes. This means verifiable damage, not neurological performance that is indicative of damage.

Brain stem: the structure at the base of the brain connecting the upper end of the spinal cord with the cerebral hemispheres. The cerebral cortex and the cerebellum and their dependent parts are excluded from the brain stem.

Bilirubin: orange-red bile pigment, occurring in the bile as sodium bilirubinate, and sometimes found in urine and in the blood or tissues in jaundice.

Broca's speech area: a portion of the left cerebral hemisphere said to control motor speech.

Bronchiectasis: the dilatation of a bronchus or the bronchial tubes.

Bronchopneumonia: a (productive) inflammation of the walls of the smaller bronchial tubes.

Bulbarpoliomyelitis: poliomyelitis (inflammation of the grey matter of the spinal cord) affecting the nerve cells in the medulla oblongata.

Central nervous system: in vertebrates, the brain and spinal cord, as
distinct from the nerve trunks and their peripheral connections (cf.
autonomic nervous system).

Cerebellum: this structure consists of two hemispheres and each
hemisphere has three lobes. The lobes differ in function, but
together they control posture and balance. Disturbances of function
lead to unco-ordinated movements, staggering gait (ataxia) or
dizziness if the vestibular pathways are affected. The 'little brain'
or inferior part of the brain lying below the cerebrum and above the
pons and medulla; concerned with the co-ordination of movements.

Cerebral cortex: the surface layer of the cerebral hemispheres in higher
animals, including man. It is commonly called 'grey matter' because
its many cells give it a grey appearance in cross section, in contrast
with the nerve fibres that make up the white matter.

Cerebral dominance: relates to the theory (originated by Orton) that
one hemisphere of the brain is dominant in controlling various
body functions. Important to many perceptual-motor theorists and
the basis for the ideas of mixed dominance.

Cerebral hemispheres: two large masses of nerve cells and fibres
constituting the bulk of the brain in man and other higher animals.
The hemispheres are separated by a deep fissure, but connected by
a broad band of fibres, the corpus callosum (syn. cerebrum; cf.
cerebral cortex).

Cerebrospinal fluid: a fluid secreted chiefly by the choroid plexuses
of the lateral ventricles of the brain, filling the ventricles and the
subarachnoid cavities of the brain and the spinal cord.

Cerebrum: the cerebrum is the main portion of the brain occupying the
upper portion of the cranium.

Cerebrum Major: portion of the brain – the two cerebral hemispheres
considered together.

Chorea: a nervous disorder characterised by irregular or involuntary
jerky movements of the muscles of the extremities and the face.

Chromosomes: small particles found in all the cells of the body, carrying
the genetic determiners (genes) that are transmitted from parent to
offspring. A human cell has 46 chromosomes, arranged in 23 pairs,
one member of each pair deriving from the mother, one from the
father (cf. gene).

Clonic phase: (in epilepsy) a sensation felt during an epileptic attack in
which contractions and relaxations of a muscle occur in rapid succession.

Clonus: shaking movements of spastic muscles after the muscles have been suddenly stretched.

Congenital: means present at birth and does not carry the connotation of hereditary or genetic.

Contracture: a permanent muscular contraction or shortening.

Corpus callosum: a large band of fibres (white matter) connecting the two cerebral hemispheres.

Cystic fibrosis: a hereditary disease of children involving defective production of enzymes in the pancreas, with disturbances throughout the body and usually with pulmonary involvement.

Deformity: refers to that part of the body already formed which has been distorted. Neither malformation nor deformity necessarily implies impairment of function.

Deoxyribonucleic acid (DNA): large molecules found in the cell nucleus and primarily responsible for genetic inheritance. These molecules manufacture various forms of RNA which are thought by some to be the chemical basis of memory (cf. ribonucleic acid).

Disability: refers to an abnormality which interferes with function to a significant degree.

Dorsi-flexion: the lifting of the foot up towards the body.

Double-blind: describing a type of study or evaluation (of drugs or medicines) in which neither the patient nor the physician knows whether the patient is receiving the drug in question or a harmless placebo.

Duchenne muscular dystrophy: a type of muscular dystrophy causing progressive weakness of the limbs and trunk.

Dysarthria: difficulty in articulation.

Dystrophia myotonia: myotonia atrophica — a familial chronic and slowly progressive disease marked by atrophy of the muscles, failing vision, slurred speech, and general muscular weakness.

Efferent nerve: a bundle of nerve fibres transmitting impulses from the central nervous system in the direction of the peripheral organs. Efferent nerve tracts commonly end in muscles or glands (usually synonymous with motor nerve).

Electroencephalogram (EEG): a record obtained by attaching electrodes to the scalp (or occasionally to the exposed brain) and amplifying the spontaneous electrical activity of the brain. The EEG is useful in studying some forms of mental disturbance (e.g. epilepsy) and in research on brain dysfunction.

Encephalitis: inflammation of the brain.

Encephalograph: an apparatus which by means of electrodes placed on the scalp records the alternating currents of the brain. It helps to find the locality of intracranial lesions.

Epilepsy: a disorder of the central nervous system marked by transient periods of unconsciousness or psychic disturbance, twitching, delirium, or convulsive movements.

Exocrine: external secretion (e.g. a gland).

Extension: straightening of any part of the body.

Extrapyramidal: the descending nerve tracts which do not enter into the formation of the pyramids of the medulla (bone marrow, spinal cord).

Emphysema: the presence of air in the interstices. Dilation of the pulmonary air vesicles, through atrophy.

Extrapyramidal system: lesions to the extrapyramidal system may lead to rigidity, tremor and unco-ordinated muscle movements.

Facilitation: making it possible to move.

Facioscapulohumeral: a form of muscular dystrophy affecting the face, the shoulder blade and the upper arm.

Fibrosis: the pathological formation of fibrous tissue in the body.

Flaccid paralysis: paralysis in which the muscles become weak, soft or loose.

Flexion: bending of any part of the body.

Floppy: loose or poor posture and movements.

Focal fit: a cortical or jacksonian epileptic fit, in which the convulsions are not general but confined to certain groups of muscles.

Forebrain: the portion of the brain evolved from the foremost of the three enlargements of the neural tube, consisting of the cerebrum, thalamus, hypothalamus, and related structures (cf. hindbrain, midbrain).

Frontal lobe: a portion of each cerebral hemisphere, in front of the central tissue (cf. occipital lobe, temporal lobe).

Gene: the unit of hereditary transmission, localised within the chromosomes. Each chromosome contains many genes. Genes are typically in pairs, one member of the pair being found in the chromosome from the father, the other in the corresponding chromosome from the mother (cf. chromosome, recessive gene).

Genito-urinary system: the organs relating to the functions of reproduction and urination.

German measles: a milder form of measles in which the skin eruption lasts only a few days and does not scale off as in the more severe form of measles. German measles (rubella) is accompanied by sore throat and fever, and is associated with enlargement of the lymph nodes.

Glial cells: supporting cells (not neurons) composing a substantial portion of brain tissue; recent speculation suggests that they may play a role in the storage of memory.

Grand mal: a complete epileptic seizure, including sudden loss of consciousness, convulsion, spasm, incontinence, and frothing at the mouth.

Haemorrhage: bleeding.

Handicap: relates to a disability which hinders or prevents what is expected or required of the child in his particular environment.

Hemispherectomy: an operation which involves the complete removal of half of the brain.

Haemophilia: a serious hereditary disorder in which the blood fails to clot and in which deep tissue bleeding occurs following injury or bruising.

Hyperactivity: overactivity.

Hyperbilirubinemia: an abnormally high concentration of bile pigment in the blood: jaundice.

Hypertonicity; hypertonia or extreme tension of the muscles or arteries.

Hyperventilation: deep breathing.

Hypoglycaemia: an abnormally small proportion of sugar in the blood.

Hypothalamus: one of the structures at the base of the brain, portions of which are significant in sleep and in emotional and motivational behaviour.

Hypotonia ('floppiness'): decreased muscle tension, preventing maintenance of posture against gravity, also difficulty in starting a movement due to lack of fixation.

Idiopathic: a term describing a disease which originates without any apparent intrinsic cause.

Inhibition: a technical term used in treatment. Special techniques of handling are aimed at stopping the spastic or athetoid patterns which prevent or interfere with normal activity.

Intracranial: within the skull.

IQ: 50-70 educable. Mildly subnormal.

Jaundice: a disorder in which bile pigment is deposited in the skin and mucous membranes, giving a yellow appearance.

Kernicterus: a condition in which there are excessive serum levels of bilirubin, resulting in brain damage. (Bilirubin: bile pigment formed by the disintegration of red blood cells.)

Kinaesthesis: sensations originating from stimulation of muscles, tendons and joint receptors.

Kinaesthesia: sense through which the organism perceives muscle movements.

Learning: a relatively permanent change in behaviour that occurs as the result of practice. Behaviour changes due to maturation or temporary conditions of the organism (e.g. fatigue, the influence of drugs, adaptation) are not included.

Lesion: a wound or injury: or, a more or less circumscribed pathological change in the body tissues.

Limbic system: a set of structures in and around the midbrain, forming a functional unit regulating motivational emotional types of behaviour, such as waking and sleeping, excitement and quiescence, feeding and mating.

Lobectomy: the removal of a lobe of an organ or gland.

Locomotion: movement from one location to another (walking, crawling, rolling).

Lumbar: pertaining to the loins, or to the lower back in the area of the kidneys.

Malformation: an abnormality of formation of part of the body.

Maturation: growth processes in the individual that result in orderly changes in behaviour, whose timing and patterning are relatively independent of exercise or experience, though they may require a normal environment.

Meconium: the first intestinal discharges of the new-born infant.

Meningeal irritation: irritation relating to the membranes covering the brain and the spinal cord.

Meninges: the membranous envelope of the brain and the spinal cord.

Meningitis: an infection of the brain and its covering membranes.

Meningocele: a protrusion of the membranes of the brain or spinal cord through a defect in the skull or the spinal column.

Meningomyelocele: a protrusion of the membranes and the cord through a defect in the vertebral column.

Modality: aspect of specific sense experience – for example, hearing, seeing.

Motor area: a projection area in the brain lying in front of the fissure of Rolando. Electrical stimulation commonly results in motor responses.

Movement: change of position.

Muscle tone: the state of tension in muscles at rest and when we move – regulated under normal circumstances sub-consciously in such a way that the tension is sufficiently high to withstand the pull of gravity, i.e. to keep us upright, but it is never too strong to interfere with voluntary movements.

Muscular dystrophy: a hereditary disease, marked by progressive shrinking and wasting of skeletal muscle with no apparent lesion of the spinal cord, the symptoms usually manifesting themselves in early childhood or adolescence.

Neural phase (in poliomyelitis): when the infection passes from the blood into the central nervous system.

Neurectomy(ies): the removal of a section of a nerve.

Neuron: the nerve cell; the unit of a synaptic nervous system. Man's brain contains billions of neurons.

Neuronic: relating to a neuron or nerve cell.

Nystagmus: continual involuntary rhythmic eye movements character-sied by slow and quick phases in opposite directions; one of the consequences of bodily rotation.

Occipital lobe: a portion of the cerebral hemisphere, behind the parietal and temporal lobes (cf. frontal lobe, temporal lobe).

Ontogeny: how an individual organism develops – its developmental history.

Operant: this gets its name from the fact that in order to obtain a reward the organism does something to its environment. As Skinner puts it, the 'term *operant* emphasises the fact that the behaviour *operates* upon the environment to generate sequences'.

Operant behaviour: behaviour defined by the stimulus to which it leads rather than by the stimulus that elicits it, such as behaviour leading to reward (syn. emitted behaviour, instrumental behaviour; cf. respondent behaviour, voluntary action).

Operant conditioning: the strengthening of an operant response, by presenting a reinforcing stimulus if, and only if, the response occurs (syn. instrumental conditioning, reward learning).

Parachute reaction: the automatic placing of hands on floor when an infant is suddenly lowered from the prone position (supported face down and horizontal).

Passive: that which is done to the child without his help or co-operation.

Periosteum: a dense membrane of corrective tissue which governs all but the articulatory surfaces of the bone.

Peritoneal cavity: the interior of the sac formed by the parietal layer of the peritoneum, containing all the abdominal organs except the kidneys.

Perseveration: continuing with a particular response after it is no longer appropriate. Inability to shift from one centre of focus to another.

Petit mal: a mild convulsive disorder related to epilepsy characterised by sudden brief blackouts of consciousness followed by immediate recovery.

Photic stimulation: stimulus produced by light.

Physiotherapy: the treatment of disorders of movement by means of physical exercises.

Poliomyelitis: an acute viral disease originating in the gastro-intestinal tract and invading the nerve cells in the spinal cord or brain stem, resulting in paralysis or muscular atrophy. A mild form of the disease may involve only fever, sore throat, stiff neck and headache.

Polioencephalitis: inflammation of the grey matter of the brain.

Polyarticular rheumatoid arthritis: rheumatoid arthritis affecting all or most of the joints of the body.

Postural drainage: the drawing off of fluid by alteration of the posture or position of the body.

Posture: position from which the child starts a movement.

Prognosis: a forecast as to the recovery or outcome of an attack of disease, based on the symptoms and the current knowledge of the disease.

Proprioception: sensation arising from stimulation of sense organ.

Prone: lying face downwards.

Pseudohypertrophy muscular dystrophy: the form of muscular dystrophy in which there is an increase in the size of the affected part due to fatty or fibrous tissue.

Reticular formation: a system of ill-defined nerve paths and connections within the brain stem, lying outside the well-defined nerve pathways, and important as an arousal mechanism.

Rhesus incompatability: that state which arises when the blood of a rhesus negative mother becomes sensitised by pregnancy to the rhesus positive factor in the father's cells.

Rheumatoid arthritis: so called because in the early stages it resembles rheumatic fever.

Rh factor' an agglutinogen first found in the red blood cells of the rhesus monkey, which affects transfusion reaction through antibody formation. Rh factor can produce antibody formation only Rh-negative blood – i.e. blood in which this factor is absent. About 15 per cent of individuals are Rh-negative and thus will have transfusion reactions from Rh-positive blood.

Rigidity: very stiff posture and movements.

Shunt: the bypassing of an obstacle in the brain by redirecting the cerebrospinal fluid through a plastic tube into another area of the body.

Sickle cell anaemia: a hereditary form of anaemia occurring mainly among Negro and Mediterranean people, characterised by sickle cells and an abnormal type of haemoglobin, accompanied by acutre and abdominal pains, ulceration of the legs, and bone pain.

Spasm: sudden tightening of muscles.

Spasticity: the state of increase of tension in a muscle.

Sphincters: muscles which open and close the orifices of the body.

Spina bifida: a congenital cleft in the bony encasement of the spinal cord, with meningeal protrusion. If the meninges do not protrude, it is called 'spina bifida occulta'.

Spino-peritoneal: as in hydrocephalus.

Stereognosis: the ability to recognise shape, size and/or weight of objects.

Steroids: complex chemical substances, some of which are prominent in the secretions of the adrenal cortex and may be related to some forms of mental illness (cf. adrenal gland). Used in treatment of some diseases when other drugs have failed, e.g. Still's disease.

Still's disease: chronic polyarthritis of childhood, with enlargement of spleen and lymph nodes, and irregular fever (after George Frederick Still).

Strabismus: failure of the eyes to converge properly on an image, leading to a squint, cross-eye or wall-eye.

Stupor (in epilepsy): a state of lethargy or unconsciousness.

Sub-cortical: beneath the cerebral cortex.

Supine: lying on back.

Systemic: throughout the whole body.

Talipes: club-foot.

Teaching machine: a device to provide self-instruction by means of a programme proceeding in steps at a rate determined by the learner; the machine is arranged to provide knowledge of the correctness or incorrectness of each reply (cf. programming).

Temporal lobe: a portion of the cerebral hemisphere, at the side below the fissure of Sylvius and in front of the occipital lobe (cf. frontal lobe, occipital lobe, parietal lobe).

Thorax: the chest.

Tonic phase (in epilepsy): unremitting muscular contraction.

Toxaemia (of pregnancy): blood poisoning, high blood pressure with kidney or liver complications in pregnancy.

Trauma: a wound or injury(suddenly inflicted).

Tremor: shaking, shivering, trembling.

Upper respiratory tracts: the air passages from the nose to the lungs, through the pharynx, larynx, trachea and bronchi.

Valgus: out-turned club-foot.

Ventricle: a small cavity of the heart or brain.

Ventriculo-atrial: referring to the operation used in cases of hydro-cephalus where cerebro-spinal fluid is passed from the ventricles to the atrium of the heart by a small tube.

Ventriculo-peritoneal: referring to the operation used in cases of hydrocephalus where cerebrospinal fluid is passed from the ventricles to the peritoneal cavity (the space surrounding the intestines).

Viraemic (phase in poliomyelitis): referring to the presence of the virus in the bloodstream.

Viscid mucus: sticky or glutinous mucus.

Voluntary movements: movements done with intention and with concentration.

REFERENCES

Abercrombie, M.L.J. (1960). 'Perception and eye movements: some speculations on disorders in cerebral palsy.' *Cerebral Palsy Bull.,* 2, pp.142-8.

Abercrombie, M.L.J., Davis, J.R. and Shackel, B. (1973). 'Pilot study of version movements in eyes in cerebral palsied and other children.' *Vision Res.,* 3, pp. 135-53.

Abercrombie, M.L.J. (1963). 'Eye movements, perception and learning' in V.H. Smith, *Visual Disorders in Cerebral Palsy.* London, Spastics Society/Heinemann.

Abercrombie, M.L.J. (1964). 'Perceptual and Visuomotor Disorders in Cerebral Palsy.' *Clinics in Develop. Med.,* II. London, Heinemann.

Albrow, K. (1974). 'The Nature of the Writing System and its Relation to Speech' in B. Wade and K. Wedell, *Spelling: Task and Learner.* Educational Review Occasional Publications, No. 5.

Anderson, E. (1975). Unpublished Ph.D. thesis. University of London.

Ansell, B. (1976). The Arthritis and Rheumatism Council Leaflet. No. 35. Summer 1976.

Ayres, L.P. (1912). *A Scale for Measuring the Quality of Handwriting of School Children.* New York, Russell Sage Foundation.

Bax, M.C.O. (1964). 'Terminology and Classification of Cerebral Palsy.' *Develop. Med. Child Neurol.* 6, pp.295-7.

Benton, A.L. (1969). 'Disorders of Spatial Orientation' P.J. Vinken and G.W. Bruyn (eds.), *Handbook of Clinical Neurology,* 3, pp.212-28.

Benton, A.L., Hutcheon, J.F. and Seymour, E. (1951). 'Arithmetic ability, finger-localization capacity and right-left hand discrimination in normal and defective children.' *Am. J. Orthopsychiat.,* 21, pp.756-66.

Biggs, J.B. (1959). 'The development of number concepts in young children. *Educ. Res.,* 1 (No. 2), pp.17-34.

Binet, A. and Henri, V. (1896). 'La psychologie individuelle.' *An. Psychol.,* 2, pp. 411-65.

Birch, H.G. and Bortner, M. (1966). 'Stimulus competition and category usage in normal children.' *J. Genet. Psychol.,* 109, pp.195-204.

Birch, H.G. and Bortner, M. (1967). 'Cognitive capacity and cognitive competence' in S. Chess and A. Thomas (eds.), *Annual Progress in Child Psychiatry and Child Development.* New York, Bruner/Mazel.

Bortner, M. and Birch, H.G. (1971). 'Cognitive Capacity and Cognitive Competence' in S. Chess and A. Thomas (eds.), *Annual Progress in Child Psychiatry and Child Development.* New York, Bruner/Mazel. London, Butterworths.

Brain, W.R. (1941). 'Visual disorientation with special reference to lesions of the right cerebral hemisphere.' *Brain,* Vol. 64, pp.244-72.

Brownell, W.A. (1941). 'Arithmetic in Grades I and II — A Critical Summary and Previously Reported Research.' Durham, North Carolina, Duke University Press.

Buffery, A.W.H. (1971). 'Sex differences in the development of hemispheric asymmetry of function in the human brain.' *Brain Res.,* 31, pp.364-5.

Buffery, A.W.H. and Gray, J.A. (1972). 'Sex differences in the development of spatial and linguistic skills' in C. Ounsted and D.C. Taylor (eds.), *Gender Differences: Their Ontogeny and Significance.* London, Churchill and Livingstone.

Bullock, N. (1975). *'A Language of Life.'* London, HMSO.

Burt, C. (1940). *Factors of the Mind.* London, University of London Press.

Burt, C. (1955). 'The evidence for the concept of intelligence.' *Brit. J. Educ. Psychol.*, 25, pp.158-77.

Bywaters, E.G.L. (1966). 'Diagnostic criteria for Still's Disease (Juvenile Rheumatoid Arthritis)', Ch. 3, *Population studies of the rheumatic diseases.* Proceedings of the Third International Symposium Congress Series No. 148. Excerpta Medical Foundation.

Caldwell, E.M. (1956). *A Case of Spatial Inability in a Cerebral Palsied Child.* London, British Council for the Welfare of Spastics.

Cambridge, J. and Wedell, K. (1972). 'When handwriting is a handicap.' *Spec. Ed.* 1 (2), pp.23-6.

Chapman, J., Lewis, A. and Wedell, K. (1970). 'A note on reversals in the writing of 8 year old children.' *Remedial Education*, 5, pp.91-4.

Chapman, J., Lewis, A. and Wedell, K. (1972). 'Perceptuo-motor abilities and reversal errors in children's handwriting.' *J. Learning Disabil.*, 5, pp.321-5.

Chazan, M. (1973). *'Compensatory Education.'* London, Butterworth.

Clarke, M.M. (1975). *Left Handedness.* Oxford University Press.

Clarke, M.M. (1974). *Teaching Left-Handed Children.* University of London Press.

Cole, L. (1939). 'Instruction in penmanship for the left-handed child.' *Elementary School Journal*, Vol. 39, pp.436-48.

Cole, L. (1946). 'The handwriting problems of left-handed children.' *Am. Psychol.*, p.456.

Connolly, K. (1968). 'The applications of operant conditioning to the measurement and development of motor skill in children.' *Develop. Med. Child Neurol.*, 10, p.697.

Connolly, K. (1968). 'Some mechanisms involved in the development of motor skills.' *Aspects of Education*, 7, pp.82-100.

Connolly, K. (ed.). (1970). *Mechanisms of Motor Skill Development.* London and New York. Academic Press.

Connolly, K. (1973). 'Factors influencing the learning of manual skills by young children' in R. Hine and J. Stevenson-Hinde (eds.), *Constraints on Learning.* London, Academic Press.

Cotterell, G. (1974). 'A remedial approach to spelling disability' in Wade and Wedell, *Spelling: Task and Learner* (see above).

Cotton, E. and Parnwell, H. (1967). 'From Hungary: The Peto Method.' *Spec. Educ.*, 56 (4), pp.7-11.

Cotton, E. and Parnwell, H. (1968). *J. Ment. Submormality*, 11,26,pp. 50-6.

Cratty, B.J. (1972). *Physical Expressions of Intelligence.* New Jersey, Prentice-Hall,

Crosby, R.M.N. and Liston, R.A. (1968). *Reading and the Dyslexic Child.* London, Souvenir Press.

Cruickshank, W.M., Bice, H.V. and Wallen, N.E. (1957). *Perception and Cerebral Palsy.* New York, Syracuse University Press.

Daniels, J.C. and Diack, H. (1964). *The Standard Reading Tests.* London, Chatto and Windus.

Dean, J. (1968). *(Reading, Writing and Talking.'* London, Black.

Deutsch, M. (1966). Nursery Education. 'The influence of social programming on early development' in J.L. Frost and G.R. Hawkes (eds.), *The Disadvantaged Child: Issues and Innovations.* Boston, Houghton Mifflin.

Douglas, J.W.B. (1964). *The Home and the School.* London, MacGibbon and Kee.

Dunsdon, M.L. (1952). *The Educability of Cerebral Palsied Children.* London, Newnes Educational.

Dutton, W.H.(1964).*Evaluating Pupils' Understanding of Arithmetic.* Englewood Cliffs, New Jersey, Prentice-Hall.

Ferrier, D. (1876). *The Function of the Brain*. London, Smith Elder.

Flexner, J.B., Flexner, L.B. and Stellar, E. (1963). 'Memory in mice as affected by intracerebral puromycin.' *Science*, 141, pp.57-9.

Flourens, M.J.P. (1824). 'Recherches expérimentales sur les propriétés et les fonctions du système nerveux dans les animaux vertébrés.' Paris, p.331.

Freeman, F.N. (1915). 'An analytical scale for judging handwriting.' *Elementary School Journal* (April 1915), pp.432-41.

Fritsch, G.T. and Hitzig, E. (1870). 'Über die elektrische Erregbarkeit des Grosshirns' *Arch. Anat. Physiol. Wiss. Med. Leipzig*, 37, p.300.

Frostig, M. and Horne, D. (1964). *Frostig Program for the Development of Visual Perception – Teacher's Guide*. Follett Publishing Co.

Furth, H.G. (1966). *Thinking without language: Psychological implications of deafness.'* New York, Free Press.

Galton, F. (1869). *Hereditary Genius*, London, Macmillan.

Gazzaniga, M.S. and Sperry, R.W. (1967). 'Language after section of the cerebral commissures.' *Brain*, 90, pp.131-48.

Gerstmann, J. (1924). 'Fingeragnosie: Eine umschriebene storung des Orientierung am eigenen Korper.' *Wien.Klin.Wochenschr,* 37, pp.1010-32.

Gesell, A. (1929). 'Maturation and infant behaviour.' *Psychol. Rev.,* 36, pp.307-19.

Gesell, A. and Amatruda, C.S. (1947). *Developmental Diagnosis* (2nd Ed.). New York, Harper and Row.

Gesell, A. (1954). 'The ontogeny of infant behaviour' in L. Carmichael (ed.), *Manual of Child Psychology*. London, Wiley.

Glavin, J.P. and DeGirolamo, G. (1970). 'Spelling errors of withdrawn and conduct problem children.' *J. Sp. Ed.,* 4, p.2.

Goodacre, E.J. (1971). *Children and Learning to Read*. London, Routledge and Kegan Paul.

Goody, W. (1969). 'Disorders of the time sense' in P.J. Vinken and G.W. Bruyn (eds.), *Handbook of Clinical Neurology,* 3, pp.229-50.

Gregory, R.E. (1965). 'Unsettledness, maladjustment and reading failure: a village study.' *Br. J. Educ. Psychol.,* 35, pp.63-8.

Grewel, F. (1969). 'The Acalculias' in P.J. Vinken and G.W. Bruyn, (eds.), *Disorders of Speech Perception, and Symbolic Behaviour,* pp.181-94. Amsterdam, North Holland Publishing Company.

Harlow, H.F. (1949). 'The Formation of Learning Sets.' *Psychol. Rev.,* 56, pp. 51-65.

Harris, T.L. and Rarick, G.L. (Sept. 1959). 'Relationship between legibility and handwriting pressure of children and adolescents.' *J. Exp. Educ.,* 28.

Harrison, A. and Connolly, R. (1971). 'The conscious control of fine levels of neuromuscular activity in spastic and normal subjects.' *Develop. Med. Child Neurol.,* 13, pp.762-71.

Hart, N.W.M. (1973). 'The differential diagnosis of the psycholinguistic abilities of the cerebral palsied child and effective remedial procedures.' *Special Schools Bulletin No. 2.* Brisbane, Australia.

Haskell, S.H. and Hughes, V.A. (1965). 'Some observations on the performance of squinters and non-squinters on the Wechsler Intelligence Scale for children.' *Percept. and Mot. Skills,* 21, pp.107-12.

Haskell, S.H. (1972). 'Visuo-perceptual, visuo-motor and scholastic skills of alternating and uniocular squinting children.' *J. Spec. Educ.,* 6.

Haskell, S.H. and Paull, M.E. (1973). *Training in Basic Cognitive Skills*. Harlow, ESA Creative Learning.

Haskell, S.H. and Paull, M.E. (1973). *Training in Motor Skills*. Harlow, ESA Creative Learning.

Haskell, S.H. (1973). *Arithmetical Disabilities in Cerebral Palsied Children. Programmed Instruction. A Remedial Approach*. Illinois, Charles C. Thomas.

Hebb, D.O. (1942). 'The effect of early and late brain injury on test scores and the nature of normal adult intelligence.' *Proc. Amer. Phil. Soc.,* 85, pp.275-92.

Hebb, D.O. (1949). *The Organization of Behaviour.* London and New York, Wiley.

Held, R. and Hein, A. (1963). 'Movement produced stimulation in the development of visually guided behaviour.' *J. Comp. Physiol. Psychol.,* 56, pp. 872-6.

Held, R. and Bauer, J.A. (1967). 'Visually guided teaching in infant monkeys after restricted rearing.' *Science,* 155, pp.718-20.

Henderson, J.L. (1961). *Cerebral Palsy in Childhood and Adolescence.* Edinburgh and London, Livingstone.

Herbert, M. (1964). 'The concept and testing of brain damage in children: a review.' *J. Child Psychol. Psychiat.,* 5, pp.197-216.

Hildreth, G. (Feb. 1945). 'Comparative Speed of Joined and Unjoined Writing Strokes.' *J. Ed. Psychol.,* 36, pp.91-102.

Hilgard, E.R. and Atkinson, R.C. (1967). *Introduction to psychology* (4th Ed.). New York, Harcourt, Brace and World Inc.

Hooton, M. (1975). *The First Reading and Writing Book.* London, Shepheard-Walwyn.

Hooton, M. (1976). Personal communication.

Hyden, H. (1958). 'Biochemical changes in glial cells and nerve cells at varying activity.' *Proc. 4th Inter. Congr. Biochem.,* Vienna, pp.64-8.

Illingworth, R.S. (1972). *The Development of the Infant and Young Child: Normal and Abnormal* (5th Ed.). Edinburgh and London, Churchill Livingstone.

Itard, Jean-Marc Gaspard (1962) *The Wild Boy of Aveyron.* George and Muriel Humphrey (tr.). New York, Appleton.

Jackson, J.H. (1932). *Selected Writings.* London, Hodder and Stoughton.

Jackson, J.H. *Evolution and dissolution of the nervous system; speech; various papers, addresses and lectures.* Vol. 2. London, Hodder and Stoughton.

Jacobson, E. (1932). 'Electrophysiology of mental activities.' *Amer. J. Psychol.,* 44, pp.677-94.

Jolly, H. (1964). *Diseases of Children.* Oxford and Edinburgh, Blackwell Scientific Publications.

Jolly, H. (1971). *Diseases of Children.* Oxford and Edinburgh, Blackwell Scientific Publications. (1973) *Textbook of Paediatrics.* Edinburgh and London, Churchill and Livingstone.

Jones, M.H., Barrett, M.L., Olonoff, C. and Andersen, E. (1969). 'Two experiments in training handicapped children at nursery school' in P. Wolff and R. MacKeith. *Planning for Better Living.* Clinics in Developmental Medicine, 33. London, Spastics Society Heinemann.

Kay, H. (1970). 'Analysing Motor Skill Performance' in K. Connolly (ed.), *Mechanisms of Motor Skill Development.* London and New York, Academic Press.

Kephart, N.C. (1960). *The Slow Learner in the Classroom.* Ohio, Merrill, 2nd Ed. 1971.

Kinsbourne, M. and Warrington, E.K. (1962). 'A study of finger agnosia.' *Brain,* 85, pp.47-66.

Kinsbourne, M. and Warrington, E.K. (1963). 'The development of finger differentiation.' *Q. Jl Exp. Psychol.,* XV (2), pp.132-7.

Kinsbourne, M. and Warrington, E.K. (1964). 'Disorders in spelling.' *J. Neurol. Neurosurg. Psychiat.,* 27, pp.224-8.

Kirk, S.A. and McCarthy, J.J. (1961). 'The I.T.P.A. – An approach to differential diagnosis.' *Am. J. Ment. Defic.,* 66, p.399-413.

Kinsbourne, J. 'Perceptual Learning Determines Beginning Reading'. Formerly of Duke University Medical Centre, Durham, North Carolina (personal communication).

Kirk, S.A. (1962). *Educating Exceptional Children.* Boston, Houghton Mifflin.

Kirk. S.A., Kirk, W.D. and McCarthy, J.J. (1968). *Examiner's Manual. Illinois Test of Psycholinguistic Abilities* (revised edition). Urbana. University of Illinois.

Lashley, K. (1929). *Brain Mechanisms and Intelligence.* Chicago, University of Chicago Press.

Lee, W.R. (1972). *Spelling Irregularity and Reading Difficulty in England,* Windsor, NFER Publishing Co.Ltd.

Lefford, A. (1970). 'Sensory, perceptual and cognitive factors in the development of voluntary actions' in K Connolly (ed.), *Mechanisms of Motor Skill Development,* pp.215-17. London and New York, Academic Press

Levin, H. (1966). *Reading Research, Why, What and For Whom?* Elementary English.

Livingston, A. (1961). 'A study of spelling errors.' *Studies in Spelling.* Scottish Council for Research in Education. University of London Press.

Lynn, R. (1957). 'Temperamental characteristics related to disparity of attainment in reading.' *Br. J. Educ. Psychol.,* 27, pp.62-7.

Malone, C.A. (1967). 'The psycho-social characteristics of the children from a developmental point of view' in E. Pavenstedt (ed.), *The Drifters.* Boston, Little Brown.

Marchbanks, G. and Levin, H. (1965). 'Cues by which children recognize words.' *J. Educ. Psychol.,* 56, pp.57-61.

McCarthy, J.J. and McCarthy, J.F. (1969). *Learning Disabilities.* Boston, Allyn and Bacon, Inc.

Mehler, J. and Bever, T.G. (1967). 'Cognitive capacity of very young children.' *Science,* 158, pp.141-2.

Milner, B. (1958). In O.L. Zangwill, 'Neurological Studies and Human Behaviour'. *Experimental Psychology,* 20, 1, pp.43-8. *Br. Med. Bull.* (1964).

Milner, B. (1962). 'Laterality effects in audition' in V.B. Mountcastle (ed.), *Interhemispheric Relations and Cerebral Dominance.* Baltimore, Johns Hopkins Press.

Milner, B. (1971). 'Interhemispheric Differences and Psychological Processes'. *Br. Med. Bull.,* 27, pp.272-7.

Morgan, L.C. (1894). *Introduction to Comparative Psychology.* London.

Moseley, D. (1974). 'Some cognitive and perceptual correlates of spelling ability' in B. Wade and K. Wedell, *Spelling: Task and Learner.* Educational Review Occasional Publications, No. 5.

Mullins, J., Turner, J.F., Zawadski, R. and Saltman, L. (1972). 'A handwriting model for children with learning disabilities.' *J. Learn. Disabil.,* 5 (5), pp.306-11.

Nelson, H.E. (1974). 'The aetiology of specific spelling disabilities' in B. Wade and K. Wedell, *Spelling: Task and Learner* (see above).

Parnwell, M. (1970). 'Conductive Education of the Cerebral Palsied Child.' *Proc. 5th Int. Congr. WFOT,* pp. 166-70.

Paull, M.E. and Haskell, S.H. (1977). *Let's Have Fun with Shapes.* Harlow, ESA Creative Learning.

Paull, M.E. and Haskell, S.H. (1977). *My First Writing Books.* Harlow, ESA Creative Learning.

Penfield, W. and Roberts, L. (1959). *Speech and Brain Mechanisms.* Princeton, Princeton University Press.

Personke, C. and Yee, A.H. (1971). *Comprehensive spelling instruction: theory, research and application.* Scranton (Pa.) and London, Intext.

Peters, M.L. (1970). *Success in Spelling.* Cambridge Institute of Education.

Peters, M.L. (1975). *Diagnostic and Remedial Spelling Manual.* London and Basingstoke, MacMillan Education Ltd.

Phillips, C.J. and White, R.R. (1964). 'The Prediction of educational progress among cerebral palsied children.' *Ev. Develop./Med. Child Neurol.,* 6,pp.167-74.

Piaget, J. (1950). *The Psychology of Intelligence*. London, Routledge and Kegan Paul.

Piaget, J. (1952). *The Child's Conception of Number*. London, Routledge and Kegan Paul.

Piaget, J. (1953). 'How children form mathematical concepts.' *Scient. Am.,* 189, pp. 74-9.

Richardson, Marion (1935). *Writing and Writing Patterns Teacher's Book*. London, Hodder and Stoughton, tenth impression 1975.

Rutter, M. (1966). 'Brain-damaged children.' *New Education,* 3, pp.10-13.

Rutter, M., Tizard, J.P. and Whitmore, K. (eds.) (1970). *Education Health and Behaviour*. London, Longman.

Schaffer, H.R. (1966). 'The onset of fear of strangers and the incongruity hypothesis.' *J. Child Psychol. Psychiat.,* 7, pp.95-106.

Schonell, F.J. (1932). *Essentials in Teaching and Testing Spelling*. London, Macmillan.

Schonell, F.J. (1948). *Backwardness in Basic Subjects*. Edinburgh, Oliver and Boyd.

Schonell, F.J. and Schonell, E.F. (1957). *Diagnosis and Remedial Teaching in Arithmetic*. Edinburgh, Oliver and Boyd.

Seebohm, F. (1968). *Committee on Local Authority and Allied Personal Services*. London, HMSO.

Sheridan, M.D. (1973). *Children's Developmental Progress from Birth to Five Years: The Stycar Sequences*. Windsor, NFER.

Sheridan, M.D. (1973). *The Handicapped Child and His Home*. National Childrens Home, revised edition.

Simpson, H. (1973). 'Asthma' in J.O. Forfar and G.C. Arnell, (eds.), *Textbook of Paediatrics*. Edinburgh and London, Churchill and Livingstone.

Skinner, B.F. (1968). *The Technology of Teaching,* New York, Appleton-Century Crofts.

Smilansky, M. and Smilansky, S. (1967). 'Intellectual advancement of culturally disadvantaged children: an Israeli approach for research and action.' *Int. Rev. Educ.,* 13, pp.410-13.

Smith, F. (1971). *Understanding Reading*. New York, Holt, Rinehart and Winston.

Smith, V.H. (ed.) (1963). *Visual Disorders in Cerebral Palsy*. London, Spastics Society/Heinemann.

Spearman, C.E. (1927). *The Abilities of Man: their Nature and Measurement*. London, Macmillan.

Spencer, H. (1870). *Principles of Psychology*. London, 1870.

Sperry, R.W. (1963). In N. Calder, *The Mind of Man,*pp.143-5.London, British Broadcasting Corporation (1970).

Strauss, A. and Werner, H. (1938). 'Deficiency in the finger schema in relation to arithmetic disability (Finger agnosia and acalculia).' *Am. J. Orthopsychiat.,* 8, pp.719-25.

Strauss, A.A. and Lehtinen, L.E. (1947). *Psychopathology and Education of the Brain-Injured Child*. New York, Grune and Stratton.

The 1944 Education Act. London, HMSO.

The Handicapped Pupil and Special School Regulations 1959. London, HMSO

Amending Regulations to The Handicapped Pupil and Special School Regulations 1962. London,HMSO.

Tizard, J.P., Paine R.S. and Crothers, B. (1954). 'Disturbances of Sensation in Children with Hemiplegia'.*JAMA,* 155, pp.628-32.

Ulrich, E. (1967). 'Some experiments on the function of mental training in the acquisition of motor skills.' *Ergonomics,* 10, pp.411-19.

Uzgiris, I.C. and Hunt, J. McV. (1971). 'Ordinal scales of psychological development in infancy' in H. Carl Haywood (ed.), *Social-Cultural Aspects of Mental Retardation*. Proc. Peabody-NIMH Conf. New York, Appleton-Century-Crofts .

Vernon, M.D. (1961). *The Psychology of Perception*. Harmondsworth, Penguin.

Vernon, M.D. (1970). Chapter 1 of *Assessment and Teaching of Dyslexic Children*. Invalid Children's Aid Association.

Wada, J.A. (1969). 'Interhemispheric sharing and shift of cerebral function.' 9th Intern. Cong. Neurol. Abstract: *Excerpta Medica, International Congress Series*, 193, pp. 296-7.

Warburton F.W. and Southgate, V. (1969). *i.t.a. An Independent Evaluation*. London, John Murray and W.R. Chambers.

Wedell, K. (1973). *Learning and Perceptuo-Motor Disabilities in Children*. London, Wiley

Weikart, D.P. and Lambie, B.Z. (1970). 'Early enrichment in infants' in V.H. Deneberg, (ed.), *Education of the Infant and Young Child*. New York, Academic Press.

Werner, H. and Carrison, D. (1942). 'Measurement and development of the finger schema in mentally retarded children: Relation of arithmetic achievement to performance on the finger schema test.' *J. educ. Psychol.,* 33, pp.252-64.

White, B.L., Castle, R. and Held, R. (1964). 'Observations on the development of visually-directed teaching.' *Child Dev.,* 35, pp.349-64.

White, B.L. and Held, R. (1966). 'Plasticity of Sensorimotor Development in the Human Infant' in J.F. Rosenblith and W. Allinsmith (eds.), *The Causes of Behaviour: Readings in Child Development and Education Psychology*. Boston, Allyn and Bacon Inc.

Witelson, S.F. and Pallie, W. (1973). 'Left-hemisphere specialization for language in the human newborn: neuroanatomical evidence of asymmetry.' *Brain,* 96, pp.641-6.

Wyke, M. (1960). In O.L. Zangwill, 'Neurological Studies and Human Behaviour' *Experimental Psychology,* 20, 1, pp.43-8. *Br. Med. Bull.* (1964)

Younghusband, E., Birchall, D., Davie, R. and Pringle, M.L.K. (1970). *Living with Handicap: The report of a working party on children with special needs*. London, The National Bureau for Co-operation in Child Care.

194

INDEX